ENDORSEMENTS

True to its title, *Mostly Unanswerable Questions* provides clarity and wisdom in an easily understandable manual for change. Lara Buelow does an exceptional job of coaching the reader on how to live authentically, embrace their inner changemaker, and ultimately transform their lives in a positive and impactful manner. Every aspect of the book provides valuable tools from three perspectives to inspire the reader on a roadmap for self-awareness and development. I highly recommend this book to individuals invested in self-improvement and all mental health professionals working with their clients. It is a wonderful resource!

Dr. Tonja H. Krautter, Psy, D, LCSW
Author of *When Your Baby Won't Stop Crying, What Every Parent Needs to Know About Self-Injury, What Every Parent Needs to Know About Eating Disorders, What Every Parent Needs to Know About Emerging Sexual Trends Among Our Youth* Private Practice, Campbell, CA Adjunct Clinical Faculty at Stanford University School of Medicine, Psychiatry Department

A fresh, fun, delightful, insightful, practical, irreverent, and unapologetically wholehearted approach to life's most common yet enigmatic questions, *Mostly Unanswerable Questions*, is a must-read for rabble rousers, idealists, and change-makers everywhere! It will enlighten, entertain, and guide you through life's often frustrating and confusing mazes, bringing you back home to yourself. Lara's uniquely eclectic and integrative lens of "Head Heart Gut," along with her Existential and Professional wisdom, gives a grounded, inspiring, expert, empathetic approach chock full of actionable resources - rare in the personal development space. If you want to make a positive impact on the world, you need this book!

Yvonne Ator, MD, MPH
Thriving Idealist
The Thriving Idealist Podcast,
Thinking About Quitting Medicine?
Yvonneator.com

Mostly Unanswerable Questions are not just any book - it's a delightful and rebellious roadmap that beckons readers to reclaim their lives from the tumultuous chaos of modern living. Lara combines her decades of experience as a professional coach with humor and practical insights, creating a compelling narrative that transcends the conventional self-help genre. The book's professional and career development section provides expert and creative guidance for those navigating the often-perplexing journey of finding purpose and authenticity in their professional lives. In a world where career choices can feel overwhelming and societal expectations often drown out individual aspirations, this section serves as a much-needed compass and is worth the price of admission.

Juliet Starrett, CEO of The Ready State, Inc.
New York Times Bestselling Author of *Built to Move*
thereadystate.com

With humor and heart, *Mostly Unanswerable Questions* is a selection of love letters to misfits and seekers. With a focus on our head, heart, gut, and existential wonderings, this book challenges you to embrace the beautiful chaos of a life well-lived...and a road seldom walked. It's a manifesto for the bold and unconventional. It's a walk back home.

Devon Loftus, Author and Writer
Coauthor of the award-winning cookbook, *The Moon Cycle Cookbook: A Holistic Nutrition Guide for a Well-Balanced Menstrual Cycle* and author of *Dwell: A Journal for Naming, Processing, and Embracing Your Emotions*
devonloftuswrites.com

In a world overflowing with how-to's and life hacks, Lara provides clarity, insight, and heart-forward direction. *Mostly Unanswerable Questions* is a great guide for those tired of being spoken to and ready to co-create a life, business, relationship... heck, an adventure aligned with their soul-self! This book will get you started on your journey with a sense of humor and self-compassion.

Winter Clark, RMMFI, Coach, Tantric Shaman
Author *of Goddess Grows Up: You Are the Gift*

Want some hot takes on self-help? *Mostly Unanswerable Questions* is a compelling and relatable guide. It's not just a book—it's an invitation to rediscover your passions, question the status quo, and live with intention. It reads like notes from a familiar and caring friend who isn't afraid to (gently) call bullshit on your default story and push you to be the truest version of yourself.

Abby Frost
Frost Wellness Group frostwellnessgroup.com

Mostly Unanswerable Questions is like a cozy coffee chat with your best friend and a thought-provoking session with your life coach with a sprinkling of Dear Abby kitsch on top. Lara's approach to life's questions reads like a quirky choose-your-own-adventure. But instead of following someone else's path, you're inspired to carve out your own. It's refreshing, quirky, and, above all, actionable.

Deanna Seymour
Graphic Design + Content Marketing
Deannaseymour.com

Lara Buelow is a rare voice. Her compassion, empathy, and groundedness come through on the page in a helpful, inspiring way and without judgment. This book is a practical guide, a therapy session, and a glass of wine with your best friend. It endeavors to help us navigate life's crossroads in a way that feels both authentic and doable, and I know it's one that I'll be coming back to again and again.

Rachel Shapiro, Tax Law

MOSTLY UNANSWERABLE QUESTIONS

Advice for Rabble Rousers
Participating in the Quiet Revolution
of Daily Life

LARA BUELOW

QUANTUM SHIFT
PUBLISHING

For information about special discounts for bulk purchases, please contact
Support@LaraBuelow.com

Cover Design by Deanna Seymour and Quantum Shift Media
Cover art by Lara Buelow

Print ISBN: 978-1-955533-24-9
e-book ISBN: 978-1-955533-25-6
Library of Congress Control Number: 2023923350

Printed in the United States

QUANTUM SHIFT
PUBLISHING

Denver, Colorado

DEDICATION

To my parents, Roland and Friederike.

To my siblings, Ben, Maya, and Salome.

Thank you for supporting me with unconditional positive regard.

Thank you for always being by my side and encouraging my creative endeavors.

I feel extremely fortunate and infinitely grateful to have grown up with a family as compassionate, accepting, and loving as all of you.

PREFACE

A dvice columns, particularly the intimate Dear Sugar and the unorthodox Savage Love, have always allured me. They fueled my aspiration to dispense wisdom to those seeking guidance.

A pivotal moment arose during an optimistic window of early parenthood when, despite the chaos of raising two toddlers eighteen months apart, I decided to go for it. I had gotten to know an author coach, Keren Kilgore, who became the conduit for creating this book.

Little did I realize the tumultuous journey ahead, testing my resilience and commitment to this passion project. Our proudest moments often demand that we summon a better, grittier version of ourselves—nothing worthwhile ever comes easy. This ethos became my guiding principle as I delved into the collaborative venture with a talented artist and friend, Hope Amico, the visionary behind the Keep Writing Project.

The quirky approach of soliciting life advice questions through snail mail postcards added a unique twist to the project. As the postcards poured in, each carried the weight of its sender's vulnerability and quest for guidance. This book is the organic result of these snail mail dreams colliding—a testament to the transformative power of collaboration, the resilience of the human spirit, and the profound impact of sincere advice exchanged in the most unconventional of ways.

I hope you enjoy the conversation.

ACKNOWLEDGMENTS

A big heartfelt thank you to my author coach, Keren Kilgore. Without your optimism, encouragement, and patience, I would never have pursued this project. Thank you for your unwavering positivity and calmness.

Thank you to my extended family, my immediate family, my husband, and my kids, who continue to love me through grueling creative endeavors and support my dreams.

Thank you to Hope Amico and the Keep Writing Project for being open-hearted, collaborative, and generous. Thanks for sharing audiences and sending so much positive art into the world. I always love receiving your snail mail.

Thank you to my postcard and question submitters! I couldn't have written this book without you. I appreciate your time, creativity, openness, and vulnerability.

Thank you to Deanna Seymour for your commitment to helping me build my brand, understanding my aesthetic, and helping me continuously get back on track with social media, email, and content creation. I so appreciate your sense of humor, sunshine vibes, and brilliant pink hair.

I want to thank everyone who believes in me and my work, especially my newsletter subscribers, my coaching clients, my mom groups, anyone who has purchased my products or art, and those who sincerely follow my social media content. There are few things as rewarding as getting sincere feedback that I make a genuine impact on your life and support you on your own path.

MOSTLY UNANSWERABLE QUESTIONS WORKBOOK

Many of the essays in this book refer to tools I use in coaching because they create better and faster results. I invite you to download the workbook and use these tools as you read these essays.

MUQWorkbook

CONTENTS

THE QUIRKY POSTCARD PROJECT

This book came to me as a vision. A snail mail endeavor, actually. It includes real people with similar passions to mine. They are creative, mysterious, and vulnerable. I have always enjoyed writing mail and maintaining pen pals. I know it has the power to touch people in beautiful and sentimental ways.

In order to write a book like the one I envisioned, I knew I had to work collaboratively with other creatives to bring it to fruition. I needed outside input. I have been a longtime subscriber to Hope Amico's *Keep Writing Project,* a monthly subscription collaborative postcard project. I immediately thought of Hope regarding this book and reached out to see if we could work together. Hope designed the postcard that featured my request for life advice questions people would like to have answered. We put Dear Sugar's quote on one side, a tribute to Cheryl Strayed as an anonymous life advice columnist. I love Strayed's work and particularly adore *Tiny Beautiful Things.*

Over six weeks, postcards rolled in. I collected the questions and began writing. To remain structured and focused, I knew I would need to write from specific perspectives. I deeply identify as an artist and as a coach. Based on these identities, I created three perspectives from

Mostly Unanswerable
Questions Postcards

which to write. The Head Heart Gut section relates to the body and spirit. The Existential perspective addresses the questions from the framework of meaning, purpose, and death. And finally, the Professional perspective provides tools, techniques, and valuable resources.

You hold in your hands the result of one woman's dream to write a quirky, artsy, life advice book.

We have the power to heal
what needs to be healed.

We have the capacity to stand
before the scorching flames &
decide what to swallow
and what to cast out.

dearsugar

life advice for those who keep trying
this is keep writing number 159, july 2022
lara buelow collaborated with us
for a special edition of your favorite monthly postcard!
lara is a regret coach, snail mail enthusiast & author.
follow her for life advice and colorful mail--
larabuelow.com and @larabuelow
keep writing is a monthly postcard from hope amico,
a visual artist & educator, who loves to ask questions.
to subscribe & receive a card like this every month,
visit hopeamico.com
or follow @keep_writing_postcards
return: po box 86174 portland or 97286

THE PERSPECTIVES

HEAD HEART GUT

The Head Heart Gut section of the response provides a conversation between these physical elements we identify in our decision-making. It gives each a voice and illustrates each one in the reflection process. This section looks at the questions received from a cognitive standpoint. It recognizes that different parts of the body orchestrate different internal conversations that are sometimes at odds with each other. In my exploration of these different perspectives, I spin a web between the parts to bring greater understanding and compassion to each.

The Head represents the rational mind, our desire to make sense of our experiences, and to explain things with logic and language. This perspective looks at how our thoughts may shape our reality, regardless of situational truths. The Head's perspective is based on internal narratives. Head is often more about societal norms, external pressure, and maintaining the status quo to remain safe.

The Heart perspective is about passion, pleasure, our personal values, spirituality, and love. A heart-centered approach to decision-making relates to what a person's values and dreams are, rather than what our rational minds would have us do to keep us safe. In the Heart section, we explore how our internal compass can often differ from the directions our Head is delivering.

The Gut lens connects us with our bodies, reminding us we are not floating heads, but a complex integrated system that is a walking-talking-feeling meat sack. The Gut leads with the intuition and wisdom of the Heart. It is always subconsciously in touch with the mind, sending important physical information to the brain, but which we often override, prioritizing our immediate thoughts and things that we have deemed productive.

EXISTENTIAL

Here, I use the existential philosophy of assigning meaning to a chaotic and confusing world to provide additional insight into the question at hand. I often bring up death, regret, creating meaning, and developing a sense of purpose to broaden the reader's sense of self and refine their inner compass. Existentialism asks for people to come up with their own definitions and understandings of purpose and meaning, rather than looking to others or institutions to provide those meanings for them. It is through the refinement of our purpose that people live authentically. Existentialism also says that existence precedes essence, meaning that an individual's life is a constant process of creating and defining.

In order to create meaning and gain a deeper understanding of the context of our life, I also write about the regrets of people who are facing death in the Existential section. Defining our own meaning of life and developing a sense of purpose is a big feat. Using death and regret, I help the reader uncover fresh perspectives and use the experience of others to further refine their own thoughts and feelings in light of their submitted question.

PROFESSIONAL

This is the coaching and advice section from a career and professional development perspective. I feel it is important here to mention my own values and approach to coaching and professional development. I am avant-garde and somewhat counterculture. I seek to revolutionize our workforce and to inspire professionals to use their actions and their work as a vote for the type of world they want to see. Change happens when more and more people say *enough*. They demand living wages, equality, better hours and working conditions. I want people to demand a better work culture and to dismantle capitalism and patriarchy in companies around the world. Obviously, this is no small task.

This section also discusses the career and professional development aspects of the questions. I use my unique coaching perspective and various trainings and suggest exercises and homework that the seeker can pursue. Through further questioning and resources, I laid the groundwork to provide a clear path forward in the professional realm. I cover coaching concepts, behavioral development, and habit techniques to move the seeker along on their journey.

A NOTE ON RHETORICAL QUESTIONS

I write this book to help people take action. Therefore, there are largely no rhetorical questions in this book. Coaching is based on asking powerful questions and playing with the clients' thinking to make space for clarity. People hire coaches to give them a fresh perspective and help them move into courageous action. I am here to provide that in written format. I encourage readers and seekers alike to approach each question with an open mind. When a question strikes you, take the time to contemplate it and write your answer. Writing deepens your reflection. When you find a question lingering or when you don't immediately know the answer, that is often when a *good* question has crossed your path. Know that not all-powerful questions are complex or perplexing. Often, simple questions that demand succinct and clear answers are exponentially powerful. Complex questions are too confusing and muddy the waters. I attempt to keep things simple as much as possible. Remember, simple does not mean easy.

Even though I am answering questions here in my book, the questions are a guided exercise in aiding you in finding your own deepest truths.

complex or perplexing. Often, simple questions that demand succinct and clear answers are exponentially powerful. Complex questions are too confusing and muddy the waters. I attempt to keep things simple as much as possible. Remember, simple does not mean easy.

Even though I am answering questions here in my book, the questions are a guided exercise in aiding you in finding your own deepest truths.

here to mention my own values and approach to coaching and professional development. I am avant-garde and somewhat counterculture. I seek to revolutionize our workforce and to inspire professionals to use their actions and their work as a vote for the type of world they want to see. Change happens when more and more people say *enough*. They demand living wages, equality, better hours and working conditions. I want people to demand a better work culture and to dismantle capitalism and patriarchy in companies around the world. Obviously, this is no small task.

This section also discusses the career and professional development aspects of the questions. I use my unique coaching perspective and various trainings and suggest exercises and homework that the seeker can pursue. Through further questioning and resources, I laid the groundwork to provide a clear path forward in the professional realm. I cover coaching concepts, behavioral development, and habit techniques to move the seeker along on their journey.

A NOTE ON RHETORICAL QUESTIONS

I write this book to help people take action. Therefore, there are largely no rhetorical questions in this book. Coaching is based on asking powerful questions and playing with the clients' thinking to make space for clarity. People hire coaches to give them a fresh perspective and help them move into courageous action. I am here to provide that in written format. I encourage readers and seekers alike to approach each question with an open mind. When a question strikes you, take the time to contemplate it and write your answer. Writing deepens your reflection. When you find a question lingering or when you don't immediately know the answer, that is often when a *good* question has crossed your path. Know that not all-powerful questions are

MINDFULNESS

the answer to this question could change my life.

Do I need to do more or less?

"Have no fear of perfection; you'll never reach it."

–Marie Curie,
first woman to win a Nobel Prize

PEOPLE SEE ME

How do people see me differently than I see myself?

Love, Yas xoxo

Dear Yas,

I imagine during your delightful years on this planet that you have asked this question many times, looking for exact feedback, and I wonder what you have learned. It is through our diversity of experience and our openness to what life offers that we learn things are not as they seem. I have always thought that if I could peek into someone else's mind for even a few seconds, that it would do one of two things. It would either alter my perception of reality so strongly that I would transform myself or I would die of judgment and a broken heart. But since I can't do that, I'll take a deep dive into my answers here.

HEAD HEART GUT

Head is filled with many judgments, most of which may even be against yourself. Head is always chatting away, judging this thing and that. Head narrates the stories of our judgments to us all day long, giving voices to people and situations as we walk through our days. Head cannot be trusted as it is completely subjective. Head wonders: *What does that Head over there see that I don't?*

Heart contains limitless compassion and empathy. Heart gets bruised and broken when Head says that Heart isn't worthy enough. Heart gives grace and has learned to love things it used to hate. It has also grown and stretched to accommodate all you have weathered. Heart knows that each of us is unique and that the world really does need all kinds of people. Heart feels into the goodness and the essence of us.

Gut has given you many snap judgments, some cruel, some kind. It has kept you safe in the face of danger and filled you in on awkward social interactions. You know those moments when you're in a social setting, maybe you are feeling confident because you're in a particularly good mood, but then you share something that lands totally flat. Gut sinks, even recoils slightly. The awkwardness descends on the scene and perhaps you fumble to repair the situation. The resulting feeling is something Brene Brown calls a "vulnerability hangover" or "shame spiral." Maybe it wasn't that bad, and it lands in the general embarrassment category. Gut weighs the thoughts, opinions, and judgments of others carefully, feeling the exposure of outside input, uncovering the answers to your question.

EXISTENTIAL

How do you see *you*, Yas?

Is this a question to spur personal growth or self-flagellation?

When you die, what legacy do you want to leave?

In what ways do you want to see yourself differently?

In what ways does gaining insight into these viewpoints shift your self-perception?

In what ways are you a beautiful, unique, and powerful being?

I see you and you are *wunderbar*.

PROFESSIONAL

The nuts and bolts of your question provide many opportunities to learn more about you and the people you choose to surround yourself with. Start with making some lists on a piece of paper. Without having to involve others in this initial round of discovery, answer the questions below.

- What do you already know about yourself?
- What kind of feedback have you received from others?
- What is it you seek to discover about how others see you?
- Where can you find professional feedback?
- How might the answers serve you?
- How might they hurt you?
- What particular encounters with others have you curious about how they see you?

If you are interested in taking this exercise out into the world and getting feedback from others, then set up coffee dates and informational interviews with one or two people you trust. This is your opportunity to try out a conversation and to see what kind of feedback you get. You want a soft start with this one. A soft start looks like making a list of people you are already close to and that you have developed trust with. Because these are such deeply personal questions, it opens you up to being extremely vulnerable, and it could backfire. A soft start is setting up an environment that is kind, forgiving, and respectful so you can feel your way into the situation.

If you're really gung-ho on this, see it as a social experiment.

xoxo, Lara

DO EVERYTHING

How do you choose just one thing when you want to do everything?

Dear Want To Do Everything,

I ask myself the same thing. The world is overflowing with abundance. There are so many activities to choose from. How could we possibly limit ourselves to just one? The research on decision-making shows us that if you have too many options, you actually have none because your brain can only juggle three to five options at a time. This is what professionals call paralysis by analysis, when we get stopped in our tracks analyzing the seven million options we see spinning around us and trying to make sense of them. Getting unstuck and choosing happens when we slow down and narrow down our options to a simple few. Let's dig in.

HEAD HEART GUT

Head sees the seven million options and gets an error message: does not compute. Head has become overloaded with information and can't make sense of a damn thing under these conditions.

Heart gets very excited amid the abundance. Heart sees a sparkle here and sparkle there - it all looks amazing and intriguing.

Gut feels the same excitement that Heart does but is reining it in real fast. It knows that there is something not quite right about the situation and is telling us we need a break to make sense of it all.

EXISTENTIAL

What is your essence, Want To Do Everything?

Do you have an inkling of what your purpose in life is?

By digging deep into your meaning of life, you will uncover a compass that holds the answer to your question. Which path forward will most serve your mission in life? Which path is one of the best expressions of your essence?

Some find meaning in pursuing many experiences during our time on earth. Some find meaning in committing to fewer experiences, but deepening the ones that they have. There are so many possibilities and ways of living. None are better than others. It is only through our own definitions and beliefs that we make it so.

When I read your question, I wondered if there is a desire that you have that scares you? Often, when we have something we deeply and truly want, it scares us so much that we feel that we have to consider other, more practical options. There are ways to combine our true desires with a life that pays the bills. We do not always get exactly what we want. However, we can find a lot of purpose in those experiences if we can illustrate its role in our meaning of being alive.

For example: pursuing a passion project on the side and working a full-time job. Sometimes not putting the pressure on a project to be our source of income allows us much greater creative freedom. When we illustrate the project as a gateway to our creative self, our moment to share our passion with the world and give it the time and space to grow into whatever it wants to be, it can free our mind and spirit in a way that work cannot.

It sounds like the desire to do everything is leading down a path of disappointment and anguish. Uncover your true desires, prescribe meaning to what you have chosen in your life thus far, and allow yourself to savor what you have created along the way.

PROFESSIONAL

If having too many options means that we have none, then it is our job to narrow down the choices for ourselves. That way, we can get a sharper perspective on all that lies before us. Plus, it is an exercise in controlling our situation and creating one where we can thrive. In this article research shows that there are two elements to deciding what we will be most happy with. One is narrowing down the decision pool to three to five choices max. Second, is believing that our final decision can not be reversed.

So, you have to set up those conditions for yourself.

Starting at the beginning: how do you choose when you want to do everything? My response to you is: you do not actually want to do everything. When you can clarify this for yourself and own it, this statement itself will help you feel more in control and confident. You could say out loud to yourself, "I am multi-passionate. I want to experience many things in life. But I know I do not want to do everything." Or "I do not want to do everything. I want a healthy variety of experiences that feed my current interests."

Clearly, even narrowing down everything to less than everything is still a lot of options. Your challenge will be to narrow your list of interesting opportunities down to three to five. And from there, choose one to start. This will be the most challenging aspect of the exercise - choosing where to start.

There are many great frameworks for making meaningful decisions. In your case, I encourage you to notice and journal about how you are currently making decisions. Pay attention to when you choose one thing over another. Take a half hour to recall when you have made big decisions in the past and how you did it. Take several minutes to relish in your ability to make decisions.

As far as choosing is concerned, also take time to think about your relationship with regret. Regret is one of our greatest teachers. Regret is a possibility when we finally choose. What we know so far about regret is that we often regret the things that we did not do over the ones that we did. So, in this case, you will likely regret not deciding to move forward more than wallowing in the options you have. You'd be better off choosing something than believing you have seven million options and continuing to analyze them. This will lead to *more* regret.

Understanding what you do not want is just as important as understanding what you do. We humans learn through trial and error and the process of elimination when we are learning about our preferences. It is the rare person who knows what they love and sticks with it for a lifetime. Use this to your advantage. Use the Define My Terms Worksheet to define *everything* (worksheets are in your free downloadable workbook). Then narrow down the items you would like to pursue to 3-5 options. Based on pros and cons, enthusiasm, resources, confidence, and other markers, you can choose which item to start with.

By choosing one path to pursue, you will learn so much.

Be brave. Be bold and choose.

XOXO. *Lara* ♥

P.S. Download the free workbook and use the Define Your Terms and the Bold Choice worksheets to help you move forward.

BETTER QUESTIONS

Why should I ask myself better questions?

Dear Better Questions,

As a coach, I know that the right question at the right time is the key to meeting you where you're at and opening up space for deep insight. There are many reasons to ask poignant questions. Sometimes uncovering your own motivations is the gateway to a life-altering experience or perspective shift.

HEAD HEART GUT

Head might be a little confused. Has Head convinced you that you *aren't* asking good questions? Head will spin you around and around a question like this one until a real and clear answer satisfies it, especially if shame is involved thinking it has asked a stupid question. Head might fret about asking the wrong thing at the wrong time - but Head may rest now while we dissect this question.

Heart says you don't need to ask better questions, unless of course, *you want to*. Heart says that all the questions you are asking are fine. More questions will come, they always do. Don't worry about it. And if better questions are begging to be asked, Heart says *I'm ready.*

Gut says...what *does* your gut say? Gut wants to sit with you. Gut knows when you are asking a big, meaty question. Gut knows when you are asking something kind of silly. Gut knows when you've landed on a question that doesn't feel quite right, but you aren't sure why. Gut is there to tell you: *keep going*.

Heart and Gut can tuck Head in for a nap and get their important work done. Head can take a break from overthinking things, while Heart and Gut work out the emotional, spiritual, and physical aspects of this question. Perhaps allowing this question to rest and percolate with Heart and Gut will bring new clarity over time. While Heart and Gut don't speak the same language as Head, they all end up seamlessly communicating when you let them.

EXISTENTIAL

What role do good questions have in your life? My work is about guiding others to design better lives, in whatever way they define *better*. This can include inspiring people to live lives that are purposeful, to believe in possibility, and to capture the essence of themselves, even just for a moment. My mission is to guide and inspire. I do much of my inspirational work through questions. Something I love about coaching is that it allows me to embrace myself as an artist but through conversation.

I have chosen to coach as a profession because it connects me to community in a way that makes me feel alive. I thrive on meaningful conversations with people. It allows me to fulfill my mission of guiding others to make purposeful change in their lives. I am always looking to ask better questions. Let me tell you a coaching secret though: most good questions are incredibly simple. And one of the most powerful coaching tools is silence.

Perhaps what is missing here, Better Questions, is having good answers to simple questions. Another piece of the puzzle that might be missing is providing space to understand your questions and answers in a more structured way. What does that look like? You guessed it: work with a coach who makes you say, "Wow, that's a good question." And then integrate your answers into your life daily. We can have big insights and then fail to integrate them into reality. Coaches help us understand ourselves and turn that understanding into an actionable value.

For example, if you deeply value family, what does that look like in your life? Is that value expressed through daily actions? And if not, what action best represents family to you? Whether it is quality time, a dinner ritual, or a weekly phone call, expressing our answers in aligned ways can bring insights full circle.

PROFESSIONAL

My purist coach is coming out to say, "stop should-ing on yourself!"

Now that that is out of the way, here is a short list of reasons why one might want to ask better questions:

- You desire better, deeper, more satisfying answers
- Exponential growth
- Accelerated learning
- More information
- Valuing good questions (if you're a coach, an open-ended thought-provoking question is like gold)

While there are many reasons to ask better questions, I am curious about your experience and what inquiry means to you. Here are some things to journal and reflect on in relationship to your submission:

- What do you seek to accomplish in asking better questions?
- What distinguishes a good question from bad?
- What are you looking to learn specifically?

As a coach, I wonder which reframe of asking better questions will pull you forward. It looks like there is an opportunity to get to know yourself more here. But regardless of which way you take this inquiry, hopefully it sounds like *I want* and *I get to* in the future.

Stay Curious,

LARA

PLAGUING ME

Dear Lara,

Anxiety is plaguing me. It comes up most nights before I go to bed and feels terrible. Sometimes it stops me in my tracks and keeps me from forward motion. Anxiety is standing between where I am and the life I want and deserve. What strategies can quench this monster?

xo, Plaguing Me

Dear Plaguing Me,

I hear you, I see you, I hold you. Please know that you are not alone. I, too, have wrestled with the anxiety beast. Sometimes it tortures me late at night into the early mornings. Anxiety is widespread. In recent years, society sees it and talks about it more, making it appear to be a growing monster. But perhaps we're simply shining a light on what's been there all along. There is relief and peace waiting to be had.

HEAD HEART GUT

Head needs to be more quiet. But how? Noise is one root of the issue. It is likely that Head is running a million miles a minute, which is an enormous source of anxiety for many of us. Head will lead you astray. Head is quick to habituate thought patterns and cycle through familiar pathways. In order to help Head rest and quiet down, it is good to practice meditation, mindfulness, or other focusing techniques you find helpful. When Head has even a few simple minutes to be more present and focus on breathing, it becomes much more peaceful.

A mindfulness practice is the time and the space that Head needs to put aside plaguing thoughts. Yes, Head will be like a chattering monkey, noticing all the sparkly thoughts that pop up. Head will say, *Oh yes! I forgot to put the milk in the fridge!* But for those precious minutes, we will watch the forgotten milk float by like a cloud. Poor Head has to hold all the to do lists, it must juggle all the planning tasks, grasp the creative downloads, and process all that is happening around you. Head becomes much more tolerable, dare I say pleasant, when we make the time to sit quietly with Head, hand in hand.

Heart and Gut say, *Shhhhhh Brain, it's OK and it's OK to not be OK.* Heart and Gut say, *Get help. Find the help that works for you.* Heart keeps the dream alive, the life you want and deserve. Heart is where all of your love lives and it wants to be utilized and expressed in the real world. Heart dreams big dreams and sends you messages about how to quench the monster.

Gut is holding the terrible stone of anxiety. Gut anticipates the evenings and the weight of all that plagues you. Gut winces and feels sick when fear stops you in your tracks, causing trembling and seemingly preventing forward movement. Gut knows that life does not always have to be this way, but also can't simply wish the plague away. Gut is also your rock of strength. With Heart and Gut by your side, you will find ways to take action and manifest the life you want. Gut has its doubts about what kind of help to seek and is open to hearing the options available and will help you make the best decision at this point in time.

You might find help in a guided meditation app, therapy, talking to your friends or your cat. Help may come as the right pharmaceutical or other anxiety reducing techniques. With guidance, intention, and a path to increased well-being, you will find moments of increased peace. Help and the life you deserve are waiting for you.

EXISTENTIAL

Anxiety is probably one of the direct results of the fear of suffering. What is your anxiety telling you that you can't quite hear or recognize? Are there secret messages from anxiety to uncover? Perhaps writing a letter to your anxiety reflecting on these questions could help you release some of it.

I have felt a sharp uptick in my anxiety since having children. I am much more likely to ruminate and imagine terrible things happening nowadays. My anxiety becomes the judge and criticizes my feelings. I lay awake in bed thinking, *Will Inez wake up again tonight?* Then my critic speaks up, *How dumb to worry about this, we will just have to wait and see.* I waste precious time that could be spent sleeping with every moment I spend thinking about this. My anxiety arrives as horrible nightmares of accidents happening to our family. It is also constantly having me assess every activity we do, like riding scooters or bikes at the playground or eating with a large pointy fork. It's exhausting.

If you are tired of being stopped in your tracks and not living the life you want and deserve, perhaps the following questions will help:

- What is it costing you to live with your current anxiety?

- In what ways is your anxiety protecting you?

- Has your anxiety provided you with any gifts?

- If you want to live with less anxiety, what kind of timeline is realistic for the treatments you would currently consider?
- Are you willing to do real work on yourself?

Wondering what I mean by real work? I'm talking about all the things I wrote above: therapy, psychiatric evaluation (which sounds serious but is literally the right medical path to getting diagnosed and exploring medication).

I am talking about exercise: it is one of the most immediate, long-lasting, serious ways to change your chemistry with so many benefits - it's a game changer. If you aren't exercising, you are working against your own mental and physical health. Walking is exercise, dancing is exercise. The real work is taking deliberate action with professional support to figure out what is going on with you specifically and what is within your control to do about it.

If you aren't ready to explore some options, then you can still go to the doctor's office and ask them for their recommendations. There are plenty of medications out there that can help us in game-changing ways. Remember, there are no magic pills - everything has side effects and a price. However, some of those are prices we can happily pay to quiet the anxiety and have a much higher quality of life.

PROFESSIONAL

Anxiety is a signal and serves a purpose. That is why it exists. Otherwise, anxiety would have been removed from the gene pool through natural selection a long time ago. How might you honor the fact that it exists? How might you love yourself even when you are anxious? My advice: Get guidance in figuring out how you want to live your life and what feels healthy to you.

As someone who has struggled with anxiety and depression my entire life, I have a lot of ideas if you are looking for some to experiment with. Here is a list to get you started:

- Meditate, I love the Headspace app, but there are many good options to choose from.

- Read the book *Peak Mind*. It's about how 12 minutes of mindfulness a day change your neurobiology.

- Check out *Struthless* on YouTube. He's a fun artsy animator who struggles with depression and substance abuse. He's written a brilliant book and has tons of great content.

- Journal! Science says that writing is a great tool to process experiences, feelings, expand our gratitude, and get a bird's-eye view of our lives.

- Talk it out, out loud. There is scientific data that talking to yourself out loud can be quite therapeutic.

- Consider traditional and alternative therapies and find something that works for you.

There are so many untapped resources out there. If you have already tried these ideas or they simply aren't ringing your bell, read *Chatter* by Ethan Kross. It's chock full of techniques to tame the chattering beast inside your head.

I am the type of person who will try just about anything to create meaningful change in my life. I have done everything from reading a dating book entitled *Calling In the One* to hypnotherapy and beyond. If you want real change, then you've got to get serious about stretching yourself. Getting a bit out of your comfort zone has proven to boost confidence, trigger awe, and increase enjoyment.

Seriously though, meditating for 2-12 minutes every single day will be one of the hardest hitting changes you can make to your brain. Science says this alone can profoundly change your life.

Another one is exercising, making sure you increase your heart rate for at least twenty minutes a day. Consistency and commitment are key. There are no magic pills in life.

Hire a coach or find an accountability buddy. Make a weekly date with yourself to check in on your plan for the week. Have an Oh Shit Plan. You can find a PDF of the Oh Shit Plan in the downloadable workbook. It is the plan you will default to when your original plan goes off the rails. Because 99% of plans do not go like we thought they would. There is always a bad day, a tech failure, or traffic waiting to happen. But most people never address this issue during their planning. So, if you struggle with any aspect of mental health, it is a great idea to have several Oh Shit plans to fall back on.

Therapy and medication are powerful support tools. I have had many benefits from therapy, but it might not be for you. It might not solve your problems right away, either. Considering the unquenchable monster that also plagues me at night, I have found Wellbutrin, an antidepressant, very helpful. I also regularly take Hydroxine, an anti-anxiety medication, to help me sleep.

My point in telling you this is that when things are rough, we need to use multiple tools in our toolbox. We need to find the ones that support us and put them to work. Usually there is no one tool that will fix all our problems. So when a therapist isn't a great fit, or the drugs aren't working the way you hoped, or exercise isn't giving you the boost it used to - find new or new combinations of tools and lean on your friends.

Go forth! This could be your mission in life - befriend the monster and quiet the anxiety so you can do your best work and show up as your best self.

Loosening the grip,

P.S. Here are the worksheets I would recommend doing (in this order) to help you move forward:

- 100 Ideas Worksheet to list 100 ways you can beat the Anxiety Monster
- Pros & Cons Worksheet to help you uncover unforeseen benefits to trying something new
- Transforming Regret Worksheet to arm yourself with inspiration and strength to take good care of yourself
- Bold Choice Worksheet to choose one of your amazing ideas
- Use the Wish Outcome Obstacle Plan (WOOP) worksheet to put a plan in place
- My Commitment Contract to make a genuine commitment to taking care of yourself because you are worth it!

Go forth! This could be your mission in life - befriend the monster and quiet the anxiety so you can do your best work and show up as your best self.

Loosening the grip,

P.S. Here are the worksheets I would recommend doing (in this order) to help you move forward:

- 100 Ideas Worksheet to list 100 ways you can beat the Anxiety Monster
- Pros & Cons Worksheet to help you uncover unforeseen benefits to trying something new
- Transforming Regret Worksheet to arm yourself with inspiration and strength to take good care of yourself
- Bold Choice Worksheet to choose one of your amazing ideas
- Use the Wish Outcome Obstacle Plan (WOOP) worksheet to put a plan in place
- My Commitment Contract to make a genuine commitment to taking care of yourself because you are worth it!

DO I MATTER?

Here is a burning thought I have: Why do I matter?

- Esther

Dear Esther,

From my personal perspective, you matter simply because you exist. However, the nuances are up to you to define. This letter gives you three different perspectives to guide you in fleshing out your own answers to this question.

HEAD HEART GUT

Head wants answers to everything. It often wants big grandiose answers, but the most satisfying ones are usually those that are simple and easy to understand. That way, Head can seamlessly integrate the reasons into other aspects of life. When Head bumps up against a meaning of life question, it can get confused if it requires leveling up, creating its own meaning, or understanding new concepts that it doesn't yet understand.

Heart says, *We matter. We are one and everything.* Heart carries the thread of connection between all existing things. Heart can hold larger-than-life ideas that contradict each other.

Heart can be compassionate and accept things it does not yet fully understand and is the pathway to always learning more.

Gut is the bridge between Head and Heart. The Gut helps the Head gather practical information that you can express in daily life. Gut feels a sense of purpose simply because it exists. However, it also wants more definition and more meaning. Plus, how do we know when we find a truth?

EXISTENTIAL

From an existential perspective, you must define why you matter for yourself. It is important that you do this because it is one of the greatest responsibilities of existing. This is what it means to be human: we get to decide what meaning to assign things. Since you exist and you can assign meaning, you matter. *Your assigning matters*.

One way to begin this defining and assigning journey is to read Oliver Burkeman's *Four Thousand Weeks: Time Management for Mortals*. Burkeman describes a practice dubbed "cosmic insignificance" in which you zoom way out on your life as a human being on planet earth. You imagine your life span compared to the creation of our universe, your problems compared to tectonic plates building mountain ranges, and ultimately, the impact any one human life may have on infinity.

Burkeman acknowledges that some may find this practice depressing, while for many of us, it is absolutely delightful and strips away much of our fussiness and feelings of self-aggrandizement. One could simply conclude that cosmic insignificance means that you do not matter. Or you could glance at some statistics of the possibility of you being you right here in this moment - that you exist is nothing short of a miracle! To read about this in simple, but mathematical language, check out *Science Alert* for a quick breakdown of how unlikely it is for you to be here with a visual graphic.

It's a fascinating thing, human existence in such a vast universe. Why do you matter? Definitely up for you to decide, since letting anyone else do it seems silly after all that math.

PROFESSIONAL

Esther, as your coach, I would guide you to fill out the Define My Terms worksheet. Check out the QR code in the introduction to download it. Then we would create a pathway to determine your purpose while turning this question into an actionable value. With the Define My Terms worksheet, you will uncover your answers to some of the following questions:

- What does *mattering* consist of?
- What examples do you have of things that matter?
- What would be proof of mattering?

These questions and this exercise create a foundation for what your personal purpose is here today. Actionable values are ways of *acting on* something we say matters deeply to us. For example, if I say that integrity is a value of mine and a reason for mattering, then an actionable way of expressing that value might be to always do what I say, to be true to my word. And when I act out of integrity, I need to clarify my speech and or correct my actions.

Another way of approaching the question of *why do I matter?* could be in the form of desire. What do you **desire** in your life? What do you desire as **proof** of mattering as a human? You could use the reframe of desire to inform *legacy*. What kind of legacy do you want to leave here on earth? Looking at people you admire and understanding what you like about them will help you understand what counts as mattering versus not.

In delightful cosmic insignificance,

P.S. Don't forget to download the workbook and use the Define My Terms worksheet :-)

MORE OR LESS

Do I need more or less?

Dear More or Less,

You know, I put this question on my Instagram story and the results were extremely clear: *Less!* Does that surprise you? Popular opinion: minimalism is so hot right now! As a self-proclaimed maximalist, my answer to your question is also *less*. But I will tell you this one thing: action leads to clarity. Taking one tiny step toward a decision will reveal additional information that may be helpful. Another way of experimenting with this is by trying on a decision for a few days to see how it feels. Pick one: More or Less - and notice what comes up for you.

HEAD HEART GUT

Head says context is everything. Head yells, *how could we ever possibly decide? We need both.*

Heart says *infinity is available to you* and cries because it knows that you can have it all, but you can't have it all at the same time.

Gut says *let's figure this motherfucker out so we can move forward*. Gut knows exactly what you need. And if Gut doesn't know exactly what you need, then pick one and see what happens.

EXISTENTIAL

Despite my attachment to your more or less drama, in the end it is up to you. Your autonomy to decide is paramount and hopefully brings you closer to your authentic self. To aid you in deeper reflection, I offer this: according to regret research, we more often regret the things that we did not do rather than those we did. Which we can turn into an interesting reflection: what will you regret more?

When it's all said and done, will the answer to this question bring definition and meaning to your life?

PROFESSIONAL

My professional suggestion is a pros and cons list. You may also enjoy the Bento Box technique. I cover prototyping in this book, which is setting up micro-experiments to try things on for size. These exercises are available to you in the free downloadable workbook. A good coach could bring you to clarity in a one-hour session. It is extremely likely that you have all that you need available to you. Take bold action and choose.

In regretful maximalism,

Lara

REAL LIFE

Riddle me this: How do you sustain the benefits of a meditation practice in real life?

Dear Real Life,

It was my understanding that, by meditating, I would receive and practice the benefits in my real life, whether consciously or unconsciously. But now that you're asking, I'm wondering if I should try harder. I have always considered the practice of meditation as a gentle but sneaky rewiring of our operating systems. How do we distinguish and/or untangle meditation practice from real life, anyway?

HEAD HEART GUT

Our modern world has done an excellent job of severing our heads from what we are: human beings with bodies. Head can have a very hard time accepting this. We aren't floating heads. We have our heads attached to our bodies. Those bodies work hard and have lots of feelings and sensations. See if you can recognize more of those throughout the day. Head is so busy all the time, it easily gets distracted and forgets about being more present. Head runs away with the next item on the to do list or the buzzing of the phone. And then, every once in a while, Head stops to take a breath, something catches Head's eye - and finds itself perfectly in the moment, sensing the movement of air, holding a cup of tea, noticing a flower.

Heart and Gut know the ways society has severed Head's connection. They are here for you, every second of every day, making sure that you are alive, that your systems are functioning, doing their best to keep you healthy. Heart and Gut are here, available to be tapped into at any moment of the day. Isn't that all a mindfulness practice is? Sitting with the body, quieting the mind, being present.

Heart wants you to speak the question out loud: "How do you bring the benefits of meditation practice into real life?" Let the question sink in. Heart loves this question and gets perky at the sound of it. Heart says that every moment is a moment to practice meditation. Heart says, *Listen deeply in conversation or to the music on the radio.* Heart says, *Look deeply into the eyes of your friend or kid, notice their hair, and their smile.* Heart says, *Tap your fingers on your skin, bring yourself into this moment.*

Gut is onboard, too. Gut says, *This isn't meant to be easy. It's a practice forever and always. A process-oriented practice.* Gut says, *Slow down when you eat and drink, pay attention.* Gut says, *I've got hidden depths. I'm always sending Head secret messages.* These messages come in the form of making decisions that feel wrong or right, the warmth of spending time with loved ones, and pretty serious dietary feedback.

Head, Heart and Gut agree: creating a moving and practical meditation that you can engage in while living your normal life is imperative. Use all your senses to make this a reality. And remember, it's practice.

EXISTENTIAL

I'm being reminded of the film *I Heart Huckabees* in reference to this question. In this black comedy, clients hire existential detectives to investigate the meaning of their lives. Watch it in response to your question. There is a scene where Albert, the main character, and the detectives he has hired are all repeating the question, "How am I not myself?" I chuckle just thinking about it - but I bring it up to ask, how are you not yourself regarding your meditation and real life? Perhaps repeating and answering the question, *how do I bring meditation into real life?* over and over will bring some enlightened insights, or at least a good laugh.

PROFESSIONAL

You have asked the million-dollar question to which I give the most boring answer: simply remembering to be present at this very moment. That is all.

But obviously, we want to dig deeper. Here are some questions that immediately surfaced for me while reading your question:

- How do you *not* bring the benefits of meditation into your life?
- What benefits are you getting from your practice?
- How do you wish to integrate them into your life further?

Here is a list of real-life benefits that I have experienced from meditating:

- When I meditate regularly, I notice I am more present.
- I am mentally sharper.

- I am physically more aware.
- I pay more attention to my breath.
- I sleep better. Meditating helps me fall asleep. I feel calmer.
- I feel more connected to myself and to everything around me: the physical earth, my coworkers, my family.

I feel more content because it gives me time to feed my introverted needs while also as a non-religious person being a way to pray in a way that feels good to me. It gives me an opportunity to send love and good vibes to friends, family, and people I don't even know (like folks in Ukraine or the refugees living at my parent's house in California). A meditation or a mindfulness practice (whatever that means to you!) makes us better humans.

Meditation is perhaps limitless in its benefits if it helps us be more grateful, more compassionate, and more helpful to others. It is time that is reinvested in every aspect of your life, even if you don't notice it. So maybe taking some time to notice how you are and are not benefiting from your practice in real life would help put it into perspective.

Your homework is to read the book *Peak Mind* by Amishi Jha. Look up and listen to the podcast episode with Brene Brown interviewing the author. It's brilliant. Amishi Jha shares her initial resistance to mindfulness training and how the benefits have completely transformed her life. Jha's entire book is based on research that shows twelve minutes of mindfulness practice a day can change your brain. That's pretty incredible. Sitting here writing about it, I feel silly that I don't spend more time in meditation. Twelve minutes sounds worth the investment.

Another resource that directly relates to your question is a book and coaching course I enjoyed called *Positive*

Intelligence (PI), developed by Shirzad Chamine. PI's entire premise is bringing mindfulness into daily life, anytime and anywhere. Since it's unrealistic for most of us to become new age monks, the PI system is based on using the five senses to practice real time meditation and being more present. If you are in the middle of a conversation with someone and notice that your mind is wandering, make a concerted effort to bring your attention back to your current engagement. You could do a ten second auditory or visual focus, paying deep attention to the person's voice or intentionally looking at their face. If you are in a meeting and find yourself getting bored, try tapping or rubbing two fingers together, paying special attention to your skin texture and sensations of touch. The idea behind PI is to find active ways to remind yourself to return to the present moment.

Another way I have heard leaders, gurus, and serious practitioners discuss bringing more present-ness into daily life is a reframe of the meditation practice itself: What makes you think that your meditation is the practice part? Meditation is the performance and everything else is the practice. I believe my first introduction to this concept was by Andy of the Headspace app. It's a way of turning your thinking on its head to challenge you to do exactly what your question begs. Bring your practice into daily life. Get creative. Perhaps you take three deep breaths every time you change rooms in your house or office. Maybe it's integrating the PI techniques into your conversations or a more concerted effort to stop multitasking in order to give tasks your undivided attention.

The resources I have mentioned in this section are very specific to your question and do an excellent job of answering it. In review: do some reflection on what's working and what isn't to get more personal intel. Next, tap some resources like *Peak*

Mind and *Positive Intelligence.* Finally, take what you learn and develop ways to be present that work for you.

In practice –

xoxo ,
LARA

CONVERSATIONS

How do we initiate real life versions of those conversations we keep having in our head with people from our past? And should we?

Dear Initiate,

This is so human!

Haha! I laugh because I can imagine others reading this and feeling seen. We can chuckle together, knowing how we all make up conversations in our minds, reminding us of our human-ness. Taking the step of initiating the conversation is a completely different reality though. And should we? The lenses below will guide you to construct the conversations you wish to have and answer whether to actually pursue them, should you wish to do so.

HEAD HEART GUT

Head says, *Here we go, let's have that conversation again... and again...and again.* Heart says, *This is weighing on me.* Gut says, *Can we address what this is really about?*

To your Head I say, *Stop it, you aren't helping.* What are you getting from replaying these conversations over and over in your head? Yes, it's a real question that I would encourage you to write about extensively. There's a lot to be learned here.

- What are you holding on to?
- What are you so afraid of?
- What are you getting out of this?
- Where is it taking you?
- What else could you be thinking or doing instead of this?
- How might you feel if you freed your mind from the conversation replay?

Unfortunately, your Head will have to be strong-armed into taking a break. Through therapy, I learned that this is called *thought stopping.* It's the same ole thing as mindfulness meditation, my friend. You hear that record on repeat; you see that convo film you've been playing and you turn that shit off. And do so as many times as you need to or are capable of when you realize it's happening.

Pumping the brakes here is giving your mind a much-needed break. We need time and space to process things. Magic can happen when we give things a rest.

To your Heart I say, *I know.* I lay a hand on your Heart and say, *It's ok. You may not get what you want, but there's freedom somewhere not too far away.*

I would love to lift that heavy weight off your heart, but it is not mine to lift. Only you can do that. There is still a process that Heart needs to go through. It may mean that Heart has a lot more pain to bear. It could mean that relief is just around the corner.

To your Gut, I lean in as close as I can to see if I can hear its musings. *Gut,* I whisper, *are you ready for this?* I laugh a little because of course it isn't! It is likely that the reason you continue to play this conversation on repeat is because there is a level of doubt, anxiety, and concern that makes you extremely nervous (or insert other appropriate feelings here). When you pursue an act that makes you nervous, your Gut gets pretty excited.

It is a push-pull here because Gut wants you to be brave, but it simultaneously wants to protect you. This is a natural human response to getting caught up in a situation where maybe you wish you had done something differently or you wish the other person had. It is a common experience to replay these things and analyze all that unfolded.

We are never really ready to do scary things and that's ok. We are (almost) always as ready as we are going to be and that's just fine. There is a thin line of fear between ready and not ready. More often than not, we are ready *enough* even though we are scared. Being scared or uncomfortable does not mean *don't do it*.

Gut can tell us valuable things in many uncertain forms. You will probably mistake Guts messages as stop signs. There are times to honor this message and times to respectfully ignore it.

One of the best examples is public speaking. Most people equate public speaking with the same amount of fear that they do death.

Another great example is asking out your crush and telling someone how you really feel about them. That is so scary! You feel it in every cell of your body. Time seems like it is slowing down and you feel everything so intensely that you may have an out-of-body experience.

That does not mean that you should not do scary things. Quite the opposite, it is *healthy* to do things that scare us. It builds character, confidence, and competency. We learn more by doing the things that make us nervous than those that feel easy. The context and the details are up to you to discern. Are you safe from harm? Your physical and emotional safety are important, so make sure to account for those. If you are receiving a Gut download that is telling you that you are in serious danger and to protect yourself, consider the level of risk appropriate to you.

The question of *should we* address these situations on repeat in our heads with people in real life - Gut can tell you. Develop your scary meter using these questions to examine the situation:

- Will addressing the conversation be immediately physically or emotionally damaging to anyone involved?

- Are you simply avoiding the conversation because you are scared or nervous? Or are there other real consequences that need to be weighed into the equation?

- How might you plan and design the conversation in a way that feels safer and more approachable even though it is vulnerable? For example, location and setting: plan on talking on neutral ground for both parties. Consider making plans with a supportive friend directly afterward. Potentially share with the person that the conversation is hard for you to have and let them know you may need to slow things down or take a break. Perhaps write out notes of what you want to say or consider doing a mock-convo with a safe buddy.

- What is the worst thing that could happen?

- What's the best outcome?

- What will be your biggest regrets if you do or do not have the conversation?

Play a game with Gut: decide to have the conversation and start planning toward it. Pay close attention to the signals Gut sends. Heart will pipe in. Notice how Heart is responding to moving forward with this plan.

Sometimes we have to do things even though they feel absolutely awful.

Heart cries, Gut shudders. We must make hard decisions.

Taking action and being an active decision maker in this aspect of your life is going to bring peace to Head. Taking the time and space to make a definitive decision on how to move forward here will free up Head's capacity for other things, bringing further calm to your body. Allow Head, Heart, and Gut to work together and show you what they are capable of.

EXISTENTIAL

You are going to die someday. The meaning of your life and all that happens in it are up to you to decide. Including what it says about you to keep having this conversation in your head without initiating it in real life.

Here are the five most common regrets of the dying:

1. I wish I had had the courage to live a life true to myself, not the one expected of me.
2. I wish I had stayed in touch with my friends.
3. I wish I had not worked so hard.
4. I wish I had the courage to express my feelings.
5. I wish I had let myself be happier.

I list these things here, hoping you see yourself reflected back to you. I would *like* to believe that we can learn from others' experiences. I hope that these five regrets give you the courage to do what you need to do in your life. The courage to live a good life and to really understand what that means to *you*.

Here are some additional thoughts:

- What are your reasons for not having the conversation?
- Imagine you were dead: would you be proud of attempting the conversation or happy you avoided it?
- What does it say about you if you continue ruminating on the conversation and take no action?
- What does it say about you if you make a definitive decision one way or the other?

Once you have journaled extensively on all the questions I have provided you here, you need to take action. Stop thinking, start doing. Just go for it. The real kicker is that the other person might not even be open to having the conversation. I pray that is not the case with you. If you are denied the conversation you want to have, your Heart may cry and your whole body will have to process and be in pain and go through the hell loop of reliving the convo over and over again for some time until the healing happens.

And that is ok, too. It is what we call life.

If someone refuses to have a conversation with you, take some time to reflect and then try to talk it out with a confidante or even with yourself. Research shows that talking to ourselves is very cathartic and can help us interrupt negative narratives in our brain. If someone denies you the conversation, know that you actively made the decision and took decisive action. You did all that is within your power and that is a beautiful, empowering thing.

Making yourself vulnerable is brave. Find resources to support your grieving if that arises for you. Brene Brown writes extensively on vulnerability, grief, shame, and empowerment. She interviews

Daniel Pink, author of *The Power of Regret*, and dives into these topics. Pink does an excellent job of sharing stories surrounding the five top regrets of the dying and categorizing further. It is a good podcast episode to listen to in order to further deconstruct these concepts. Finding fresh perspectives and reflecting on your domain of control through personal narratives or stories are excellent tools for processing difficult feelings.

That said, it seems fairly likely you will get a conversation out of it.

Imagine what you might learn in the process of trying, doing your best, and staying true to your Heart. Life will not last forever. You do not have infinite chances to check in with people. You do not know how they will initially respond, but you also do not know what doors it may open beyond your initial interaction.

PROFESSIONAL

If you are interested in initiating the conversation that you continue to have in your head, I have written a short and simple message here to help you do so. You can copy and paste this as an email, text, or phone call script and send it to the person you desire to reach out to: "Oh hey friend [their name], how are you? I would love to schedule some time to catch up. Do you have time this week?"

Or if this is not a friend and someone in a more professional context: "Hi [name] it's me [your name]. Do you have time for a half hour call this week or next? Looking forward to hearing from you. All the best."

Adding a time frame is super helpful. Depending on your relationship to this person and what you're going for, a 20-minute call, an hour, or a response by a certain date gives people structure and accountability. Context is everything!

Scheduling conversations is the easy part. It is the *having* of the conversation that can be a real doozy. Should we initiate these things? You are asking a self-help obsessed artist life coach. My answer is enthusiastically YES!!!! It is a hardcore YES. Initiate, get support, have the conversation, reflect on how it went. Get more support.

This script will help get the conversation rolling as to when and where you are going to speak to this person. Once you have something on the calendar, that will be your timeline to prepare. It's a form of accountability. The next step is following through with it. Go back to the Head, Heart, and Gut section to consider how to take care of yourself if this is a high stress interaction. How can you best prepare? Write out a plan. Bonus points if you get yourself an accountabili-buddy. Find a friend or family member who can help you prep and debrief on how it all goes. And that's about it, sweet cheeks.

Action leads to clarity. And it sounds like you need clarity. If a conversation with the actual person seems too hefty to start, why not bounce the idea off a confidante? Do you have a sister to call? Mom? A BFF? A coach? Perhaps voicing some things out loud will take the charge out of some of what is going on. Voicing things out loud is incredibly powerful and transformative.

Practice!

On another note, have you seen the show *The Rehearsal*? It is an entire show based on this question. *The Rehearsal* is a docu-series by Nathan Fielder where he gives people the opportunity to rehearse their own lives, to practice doing exactly what you have described. Fielder goes to incredible lengths to allow ordinary people to play out certain big-moment scenarios in their lives. In the initial episode, Fielder helps an awkward trivia buff plan out a difficult conversation where he wants to uncover a lie between him and a longtime friend that has been weighing on him for years. Throughout the rehearsal process, they cover all possible scenarios in the unfolding interaction. It is an awkward, unnerving kind of show, but it may also inspire you on this journey and it is definitely good for a few laughs.

Be brave. Be bold. It will not go unnoticed by the universe or those around you.

Sincerely,

RELATIONSHIPS

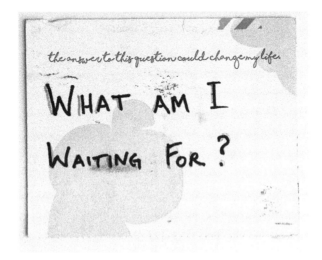

the answer to this question could change my life.

WHAT AM I
WAITING FOR?

Plant seeds in the cracks of your broken heart and
pray for rain.

-Andrea Gibson

TRUE TO MYSELF

How do I remain true to myself while living a life deeply intertwined with others?

Dear Deeply Intertwined,

As a mom of two toddlers, eighteen months apart, your question lands *hard* with me. Even though I do not know your situation, I feel the significance of being part of other's lives, the responsibility, the consideration, and the complexities of the intertwined-ness.

HEAD HEART GUT

Head rattles around this question, like someone sorting through a junk drawer. Head always believes that it can think its way through anything. That would be nice if it were true, but it is not. Head will help you integrate what your Gut and Heart already know to be true. To help Head feel useful (Head always wants to feel useful), write down everything that Head says. That will help Head quiet down a little so we can let Heart and Gut speak. Once our body has spoken, we can use Head again to integrate what we have learned.

Heart does not want to be forgotten. Heart is reminding you that there are certain parts of yourself that are yearning for more time, attention, and love. Heart says, *I am here! Let me out! Express me!*

Gut feels you so deeply. Gut knows how important it is to care for others. Gut knows that all the caring that is done is what makes the world go around. Gut knows that being deeply intertwined is the lifeblood of humans. Gut also knows, holding hands with Heart, the struggle of independence vs. interdependence or community. To feel love and contentment, we want and need to deeply intertwine. We also want a certain level of autonomy and freedom. We need to honor the different aspects of ourselves, the different expressions that the soul yearns for to feel fully expressed in life.

EXISTENTIAL

Deeply Intertwined, life is meaningless unless we assign it meaning. When you deeply intertwine with others, you derive much of life's meaning from them. Existentialism says that you are responsible for defining the meaning of life and for prescribing your own essence. The idea behind essence is that we are all born with one, a thing that is a part of us that determines what our life is about. Essence is your nature, which is developed by your experiences and actions. Existentialism came around and said, "Yes, we have an essence, but it is not predetermined before birth." When we come into the world, we get to determine and define what our essence and our purpose here is.

Notice that I said *we get to*. It is an opportunity that we each have. But no one is going to force you to do it. Existentialists say it is imperative that each human decide and determine their own essence. That practice is in good faith. We must do it for ourselves authentically. What the existentialists mean by authentically is that we aren't blindly accepting beliefs, definitions, vocations, and ways of living our lives from others. If we adopt the beliefs, meanings, and definitions handed down to us by parents, bosses, companies, politics, and the norm of whatever culture we live in, then we are taking the easy road.

I read your question as a question of essence. This is no small thing to define our essence.

All the exercises in the professional section are aimed at helping you define what your essence is and how to honor it. Here are some additional journaling or meditation questions to get you the answer you seek:

- In what ways are you untrue to yourself and what makes that so?
- What truths are you certain about in your life?
- Even when we are doing things we do not enjoy, how can those actions support our essence or further develop our purpose in life?
- What is the purpose of hardship, evil, violence and other difficult human experiences?
- How can we integrate good, bad, and the rest into our meaning of life?

Deeply intertwined, I believe you have deep roots. I sense that your essence has much to say. I am excited for you to do all that calls to your true nature. Write me another letter and let me know where your essence takes you.

PROFESSIONAL

My dear Deeply Intertwined! Together, we will carve a path that will lead to a meaningful answer to your question. Here are the steps we will cover together:

- Define your terms
- Immediate action questions
- Commitment Contract
- Good Time Journaling from Designing Your Life (a deep schedule review)
- Creating rituals and scheduling time to honor yourself

We begin by defining what *remain true to myself* means to you. Download the free Workbook and fill out the Define My Terms worksheet.

Once you know what being true to yourself looks like, we can begin putting it into deliberate practice. To get started on this work right away, look at how you have defined being true to yourself. Answer the following questions and then fill out the Commitment Contract to start making real change.

- What actions can I or do I take that make me feel true to myself?
- What is one small thing I can do to instigate this feeling?
- What is the two-minute version or two-minute exercise I can do to feel true to myself even in short moments?
- When I am feeling overwhelmed, what can I tell myself to remember that I am in the process of being more true to myself?

With the answers to these questions, fill out the Commitment Contract to yourself (in the downloadable free workbook) as specifically as you can. Put it in a place where you will see it every day or use the My Roadmap worksheet as a visual reminder. Keep your two-minute *being true to myself* exercise in mind.

To take this information deeper, you can do the Good Time Journal from *Designing Your Life*. This journal exercise guides you through a time audit of all the activities that you do within a week. This is a detail-oriented activity to build a library of understanding around what you do, when you do it, what feelings those things bring up, are they draining or energizing, and what you can do about all of that information, if anything.

Once we have an accurate time map of what a typical week looks like in your life, we can put a plan in place to maximize what feels good, giving you a greater sense of being true to yourself.

When I read your question, I do wonder what is missing from your day-to-day that makes you feel you are *untrue* to yourself?

In coaching sessions with clients, I regularly ask about what is missing. Often when we are searching for change or transformation, it is hard to know what we are lacking. However, we need to make distinctions about what is missing from our lives to understand what is working and what we need more of. If you feel like there is something missing from the work above, name it now. Then do the immediate action questions again.

The final step in our process is to expand on the immediate action questions by creating your own ritual around being true to yourself. By ritual, I simply mean scheduling your special activity to feel true to yourself into your weekly life.

A common complaint and problem I come across is that people don't want to activate or plan the moment; they simply want to be inspired to have an X feeling. An example that comes to mind is creative practice. I have heard many friends and clients say they don't want to plan making art, they simply want to feel inspired, naturally, without prompting. I very much relate to this feeling. However, if you are spending your time waiting for inspiration to show up and it never does, you never get to the activity that you are actually yearning to do. So, you have to show up and go through the motions. It is often when we are going through the motions, doing the work, that inspiration arrives or at the very least plants some seeds.

I must show up in the studio and do the painting and the drawing. James Clear in *Atomic Habits* connects habits and identity. Doing the painting is a vote toward my identity as an artist, which makes me feel good. This good feeling fuels my inspiration to continue making art and as I create more art, I create a body of work. My body of work inspires new ideas that lead to me making even more work and bolsters my identity as an artist. Around and around the cycle goes. To tie this back to feeling true to yourself, perhaps you need to intentionally create moments to practice this before it can arise on its own. Danielle LaPorte in her work *The Desire Map* shows us desire can be our compass. By doing specific actions that help you cultivate the feelings you want, you begin to feel it more in other parts of your life. Ritualizing, scheduling, making the moment special for yourself will help make it a time that you look forward to and enjoy. These things make it more likely that you will continue practicing them.

Here are the elements of success to being true to yourself more regularly moving forward:

- Have a two-minute version of something that makes you feel true to yourself. You will get busy, tired, overwhelmed and you need a no excuses version of your thing so that you can do it wherever and whenever you can.

- Schedule time weekly to do the things that make you feel true to yourself. What is the window of opportunity to sink deeper into being true to yourself? How much time can you schedule? What can you realistically accomplish and enjoy in that time?

Now go forth, be true to yourself by putting these things into action.

In Essence,

WHAT IS MINE

How do I know moment to moment, day-to-day, what is mine as opposed to what I carry from parents, ancestors, and society?

Dear What Is Mine,

My immediate reaction to this question is *Ah! Shit.* This comes from a place of sincerely wanting to give a good, clear answer that is helpful. At the same time, I have an intense feeling that yells, *We will never know! This is one of life's unsolvable mysteries and it's not fair!* It is worth it, however, to do some digging and see what answers you can come up with for yourself.

HEAD HEART GUT

Head will do its best to sort this out for you. Head wants to tease out all the details and the intricacies of your life, your past, your history. Head wishes this was a puzzle it could simply put together. Unfortunately, the level of complexity in answering the question *what is mine?* is so intense that any answer could change, evolve, or dissolve over time. Lucky for Head, we can feed it some answers that will satisfy its thirst for knowledge.

Heart weighs heavy under this question and even heavier under the knowledge of what came before it. Heart carries with it the ancestors, the parallel lives, and the lives lived before this iteration. Heart weighs heavily under society - the drama and the politics that get in the way of what Heart was built for, which is love, of course. Heart can stand tall and show off its resilience and strength. It was born out of everything that came before it.

Gut hangs in the balance of what is yours and what you carry from external influences. Gut stands at the intersection of *me* and *society*, which can be quite confusing. Gut may find the burden of responsibility and shed the weight of ancestral trauma answering this question.

EXISTENTIAL

Your question and its answers could be a summation of the existentialist task of defining the purpose of life for yourself and the meaning of all things that you assign importance to. The existentialist would say that this question is the path to understanding your true, authentic self. Awareness allows us to ask questions and seek answers. But because we are anti-shoulding (don't *should* on yourself), we reword that: it is our duty to do the work that calls to us during our time here on earth. By doing the work, we free ourselves. And in freeing ourselves, we give others permission to pursue a similar path, answer similar questions, and to free themselves.

In other words, existentialism says you are a free agent - your past or your heritage do not define you. It is your choice to continue to be defined by your past and it is your duty to own your circumstances.

PROFESSIONAL

As a coach, my knee jerk reaction is: With lots and lots of therapy and lots of reflection. Sometimes discovering and knowing your zone of control is easy. Sometimes it requires deep introspection.

Doing serious digging into this question, figuring out what your blind spots are and how your ancestral history influences you, is something therapy would be a good place for. A simpler starting point is dissecting your life as it comes up right here and now. When you catch yourself feeling coerced or *shoulding* on yourself, stop.

Here are some questions to disentangle what is yours and what is not:

- Identify the pressure you are feeling. Where is the *should* coming from?

- What is the story you are telling yourself that is causing that feeling?

- Get in touch with where you are right now. Where do you want to go? What is the next step you want to take to get you there?

Take this reflection exercise further with *The Work* by Byron Katie, who elicits deep insight with these four questions:

- Is it true?

- Can you absolutely know that it's true?

- How do you react when you believe that thought?

- Who would you be without the thought?

After answering these four questions, come up with a turnaround, a sentence that is the opposite of the original statement you made. Repeating this exercise around conflicting thoughts or intense feelings can be immensely helpful in unraveling personal truths.

Here are some professional coaching exercises to continue your work to identify what is your personal responsibility:

- Fill out a Wish Outcome Obstacle Plan (WOOP) worksheet (in your downloadable workbook) to reveal what it is you wish to accomplish in answering this question and to build a plan to get you real answers.

- Write a list of what you seek to let go of: you can use the 100 Ideas List (in your downloadable workbook) or simply brainstorm in your own fashion.

Start reading books on healing generational trauma. There are many reading lists out there with strong recommendations: google *healing generational trauma reading list*.

In order to take personal ownership to its furthest limits, it requires shifts in your perspective and allowing in new information. But the real meat of this question requires you to go much deeper and having a guide will make that easier. Couple this with therapies, knowledgeable people and resources such as somatic techniques, hypnotherapy, behavioral counseling, or a guided mushroom journey to unpack this. In this day and age, you can find coaches, witches, psychics, therapists and more to help you understand yourself. What other information or experiences could you be open to?

Through the accumulation of knowledge, you will find the answer to your question, dear What Is Mine, and you will be set free.

Untangling,

LARA

SEXUALITY & SPIRITUALITY

Lara,

What's the relationship between sexuality and spirituality? What do these two energies have to teach us?

Love, Jay

Dear Jay,

Personally, I believe that sexuality and spirituality have a very intimate relationship. This question screams, *why are we not learning about this from the day we are born!* These questions define our very existence.

HEAD HEART GUT

Head knows that there is a synergistic relationship between sexuality and spirituality. However, Head often has a hard time conceptualizing these complex ideas and likes to compartmentalize when it can. It would rather stereotype or put people in boxes. Head needs to connect deeply with Heart and Gut to uncover its own truth.

Heart is where the relationship between sexuality and spirituality blossoms. Heart allows the complex nature of both to grow and unfurl in its myriad and mysterious ways. Heart wants us to learn about sexuality and spirituality so that Head can celebrate the physical benefits.

Gut nudges you that the strong connection between sexuality and spirituality can be scary and controversial. It knows that despite social and cultural influences, it needs to build its own compass and decide what to keep and what to discard. Gut is letting you know when to push forward and expand your comfort zone and when to slow down and integrate the information you're receiving.

Live in the Heart as much as possible to strengthen the bridge between sexuality and spirituality. Channel what you know to be true through the Gut. The Head is ever present and a complete monkey mind. Get Head in the game to strengthen the sexual-spiritual connection. This is not a simple or easy question. It will require connecting the mind and the body in new ways.

EXISTENTIAL

The concepts of sexuality and spirituality are both fluid and complex. The lessons they have to teach are small pieces of a vast picture. What seems most important in this question is to define each piece for yourself and create a collection of stories, experiences, and philosophies to build them out. A good place to start is teasing apart what religion, politics and culture have taught you versus what you believe as an individual.

The reason societal pillars like religion, politics, and culture are important is that they are steeped in tradition and often attempt to control individuals through profound aspects of human experience, particularly sexuality and spirituality. Plus, these pillars are so deeply integrated into our experiences that it is challenging to pull them apart.

However, the crux lies in realizing that no universally correct or incorrect interpretations exist. Instead, both sexuality and spirituality are deeply personal, open to individual understanding and exploration. The richness of human experience lies in the diverse tapestry that contributes to our evolving comprehension of these concepts.

In essence, the interplay between sexuality and spirituality lies in embracing the fluidity of these constructs. They elude rigid definitions imposed by external entities, beckoning us to embark on a mind-bending journey of self-discovery. The quest becomes about bucking societal expectations and unraveling the intricate layers of personal meaning within the words sexuality and spirituality. The true essence of these concepts lies not in adherence to external norms but in the individual's evolving relationship with them.

PROFESSIONAL

I won't lie to you, Jay. I have never formally laid out my thoughts on the intersection of spirituality and sexuality before. Though I considered becoming an erotic novelist briefly. I have explored my sexuality in a variety of ways. Though the question of spirituality is one I continue to chip away at.

As a coach, my strategy would be twofold. One, to dissect your question further by probing your motivations and curiosity. Second, to come up with actionable items that could exponentially expand your answers. These questions are worthwhile. I think these things have the potential to increase the quality of your life. So, as a coach, I would say, find a guide, a mentor, a confidante who can help you level up in this realm.

Google and Oxford Languages define sexuality as "the capacity for sexual feelings" and "a person's identity in relation to the genders to which they are typically attracted." Those definitions feel a bit lacking to me. I like this description by Better Health: "sexuality is about your sexual feelings, thoughts, attractions, and behaviors toward other people. You can find people physically, sexually, or emotionally attractive and that is all part of your sexuality."

What is spirituality? According to Dr. Maya Spencer, "Spirituality involves the recognition of a feeling or sense or belief that there is something greater than myself, something more to being human than sensory experience, and that the greater whole of which we are part is cosmic or divine in nature."

For my personal pursuits in deepening my understanding of spirituality, I've been reading books like *Soul Pancake* by Rainn Wilson and *Spirituality for Dummies*.

It is my belief that spirituality and sexuality are deeply intertwined and that we must cultivate a deep understanding of both to truly understand ourselves. There are many religions and philosophies that have practices around deepening spirituality and sexuality together. Of course, there are plenty of religions and beliefs that state that sex and sexuality can only be honored within a marriage. As an open-minded modern western woman, I am interested in expanding the ideas behind sexuality and spirituality. I desire a world that creates dialogue and openly shares the knowledge of both realms. I do not believe in shaming individuals around their sexuality or sexual practices, as long as they are consensual.

In *Soul Pancake*, Rainn Wilson calls for a spiritual revolution. The idea is that religion and spirituality are not negative; they are positive and even essential in a person's life. Therefore, we must strive to increase our sense of justice, service, and togetherness through spirituality worldwide.

In that same vein, I believe this extends to sexuality and is naturally incorporated in the revolution Wilson calls for.

Perhaps the necessary next step in spiritual evolution is to be open and accepting of sexuality. This would allow us to transcend the suffering and control we impose on others based on sex and personal expression. This would create a more just and equitable world.

Here are more steps to further develop your own answer to this question:

- Think of a sexual or spiritual experience you've had that felt transcendent. How did that influence your spirituality?

- In what ways does your sexuality define who you are? How has spirituality influenced this?

- How do your feelings of love toward others deepen your understanding of love itself, connection and oneness?

- What do you know already about the energies of spirituality and sexuality? What are you looking to learn?

- What resources can you seek out to find more answers to your questions?

Jay, this is the kind of question that no one has the right answer to and where the answers always seem to be expanding. This is a great question to explore through coaching! Consider seeking out a spiritual guide or sexuality coach. I hope your journey creates opportunities for expansion.

At the intersections,

Lara

WHERE TO PUT ROOTS

Should I stay in New York and build my life here or move back to Colorado to be closer to my side of the family?

Dear Where to Put Roots,

Move closer to your side of the family! I'm kidding! Kind of! It depends! I'm biased!

This is an excellent question and one many of us ask regarding family/friends. It has a lot of practical exercises to find answers. It is also a big decision that will likely require the input of other parties (say, a partner, family members, work, etc.) For this reason, where to settle can be a very tricky question. As lovely as our global world is, we still need close-knit communities and places that feel like we are at home, with family to feel whole, to feel human. If New York makes you feel at home, then it is a good choice. If you can grow and embrace your life in New York, do so wholeheartedly and you will reap the rewards.

HEAD HEART GUT

Your Head already has a pen in hand and is ready to go for the pro and con list! Let's solve this problem. To go along with Head, gather those writing materials and get scribbling. Head is the one working numbers, checking flight prices, keeping tabs on the family in Colorado, and contemplating which would be *better* in the long run.

In a world that is increasingly global, Heart wants community. Heart wants to feel safe, connected, and seen. Heart wants to feel at home. Heart may sense the possibility of regret if it doesn't make an active decision one way or the other. Maybe Heart is homesick or missing family members. Or maybe Heart has nestled into its new home in New York.

Gut might already know the answer to this question. If Gut has already decided or has been in the know all along, then it will likely show up as you choosing one answer and uncovering where your true feelings are. This looks like saying, "I will put down roots in New York" and either feeling content or your Gut saying, *Oh hell no!* Committing to decisions for short periods of time can be a great tool to uncover what Gut knows.

Just because Gut knows something though, does not mean Head does. Gut understands how tricky answering this question could be. Gut knows that some strong negotiation may be necessary. Gut is also aware that it would like to spare itself the big R (regret) if it can help it.

EXISTENTIAL

Journal and meditate on the following questions. You could also uncover the answers in conversation with a friend or coach.

- How does New York make you feel?
- What is your Gut telling you?
- Could you die happy there?
- What regrets factor into this equation?

Many people claim locations call to them through dreams, through spirit, or otherwise. Some people feel immediately connected to a place. Some never do. I remember when I visited Bellingham, Washington for the first time to visit Western Washington University. I was trying to decide whether I should transfer there for the rest of my college education. The landscape was stunning, and I was lucky to be paired with a current student who was friendly and inclusive. We spent the evening with a group of students, riding bikes through town. I felt like Bellingham spoke to me then. It said that I could build a home there and enjoy a life of adventure. And that's exactly what I did between 2008 and 2011. I continue searching for physical locations to speak to me. I yearn for the feeling of home and meaningful connection. Sometimes you get to make location decisions based on a good match, other times you prioritize a partner or an opportunity.

What's your story in New York?

Here is another assignment: write two stories. One in which you stay in New York forever, the other in which you move back to Colorado. See what comes to you as your narrative unfolds.

PROFESSIONAL

From a professional standpoint, we need to lay out the various categories that influence your decision, determine how they factor into the answer and weigh each item. There are also several excellent decision-making tools that you can employ. The Bento Box technique, for one, would provide a good perspective. For all the details about Bentoism, visit https://bentoism.org/2-the-bento-method

Bentoism and specifically, the Bento Box technique, is using a four-box grid to reflect on the following categories of decision perspectives: *present me, present we, future me, future we.*

Let's use moving as an example: Should I stay in New York? Now write about the different perspectives to gain more insight into what factors into this decision.

Now me may already be ready and willing to move back to Colorado. *Future me* is extra ready to move because you think you want to have a baby and have your family's support. *Now us* would like to move but doesn't feel ready because of employment and housing opportunities. *Future us* is getting everything lined up to purchase a home in Colorado and making the arrangements to make it happen.

The Bento Box can clarify things personally and professionally. What is your career and professional development calling for? The professional landscape continues to shift quickly. Many more of us can work remotely now and make adjustments based on location.

You have got to think through your priorities and make the best decisions you can based on those moving forward. The professional career world will always be here, waiting for you. That is not the case with family.

The Harvard Study of Adult Development research article states that high-quality interpersonal relationships are extremely important to our well-being and our happiness. There are actual mathematical equations you can run to determine the number of days you have left with your loved ones. If high-quality relationships are essential, it would be imperative to maximize your time with the people you say are so important to you and to cherish the moments you have. Regret research teaches us that most people do not lie on their deathbeds wishing they had spent more time working. Being gifted with these insights, how does that influence your career decisions?

The bottom line is that you do not have forever to spend time with friends and family. You have limited time. Work is not your family, and that is an important boundary for all parties. If friends and family are a big part of your life, then factor that into your decision.

What's stopping you from having a clear answer to this question? Write it all down, start there.

Courageously,

P.S. A note on decision making and happiness or satisfaction. Research says that you will be the most satisfied and therefore happiest making a decision you believe cannot be reversed. If you are too stuck to make a decision, I advise trying on decisions for size before making a big intentional decision. Prototype what one decision would look like and live it out for a few days. As you gain clarity through action, make a point of making an intentional bigger decision and commit to it fully.

GUILT

Will I be able to get past the guilt I feel around not being there to help my family, my mom in particular?

Dear Not Being There,

EEK.

My initial knee jerk response is, "Probably not." And then I want to immediately retract that because the healers and teachers I have come across over the past few years teach everything is healable. I do not know what your experience with letting go and healing is, Not Being There. For me, these journeys have been grueling; riddled with grief, overwhelmed by stubbornness, and often completely confusing. That said, I am simultaneously in the anything is possible camp.

HEAD HEART GUT

Head keeps asking this question, rolling it around in the mind again and again. Head wants a neat little answer that fits on a postcard. Head also spirals out of control until the wee hours of the morning, worrying about Mom.

Heart cradles guilt in its warm hands. Heart holds on to guilt because it is so full of love for Mom. It worries for Mom. Heart's worry is an expression of the love it has. Heart says *yes, I can let go of the guilt.* Heart unfolds and expands in all the ways you can imagine and more when you do the work that Heart asks you to do.

Gut feels sick with guilt. Gut knows the damage that guilt can do to the body and the mind. Gut says, *be careful! It is the body that keeps the score.* Gut says, *we can process this, digest it fully.* But remember, Gut is one part of an entire system and digestion takes time.

EXISTENTIAL

Our bodies weigh so heavily with our intense feelings around family. Especially with our parents. It can feel impossible to let go of guilt and sadness connected to lost opportunities or not being able to serve someone dear to us.

I say probably not, but it isn't impossible either, because the thought of familial and generational guilt seems so gigantic and insurmountable to me, so cyclical and complex, that I am immediately overwhelmed and think, *letting that go sounds like magic.* But that is a naïve and small-minded approach. What keeps me going in search of answers to questions just like this one is the abundance of the world. There are weird and wonderful things available to us humans, and some of those involve letting go of deep guilt, trauma, and sadness.

Outside of journeys to heal whatever struggles we deal with, here are some questions that hopefully will uncover a new perspective or approach to your situation:

- Have you had a heart-to-heart with your mom about your feelings?
- Have you discussed what it's like for her to not have you around?
- What are the pros and cons about not being around?

Engaging in conversation can have a deeply therapeutic effect. It's a rare thing to truly uncover the nuances of our feelings. It's freeing to talk out our heartaches. Perhaps there is space for you to reframe your guilt. The underlying message I am hearing in your question is "I love my mom and I would love to express that by caring for her more in person. I love my mom and I will always have a desire to care for her and return love to her in that way."

With the frame of death around it, what would you consider enough time spent with your mother before one of you leaves this earth?

Is it ever enough?

For some, there is a clear line between not enough, enough, and too much. For others, it's so blurry and pixelated we may never know the distinctions. It's hard to imagine mothers dying and there not being some regrets, sadness, and guilt being left behind. And that's OK. Because in some ways, it would simply be so weird, so un-human to *not* have those things. It would almost be rude. It's an indication of depth, intensity, and opportunities for growth.

PROFESSIONAL

I imagine many a practiced therapist and spiritual healer (among others) would argue yes, you can get past the guilt you are feeling. I'd encourage you to have that conversation with one of them. There is always a lot to uncover in the mother-child (parent-child) relationship. It is always fruitful to reflect on and to channel whatever you learn into your life moving forward.

As a coach, I would gently remind you of the distinctions between coach and therapist. Then I would turn the question back around to you:

- What have you already tried to process the guilt you feel about not being there for your mom?
- What's stopping you from letting go of the guilt?
- What other options are available to you to work on this?

I recommend therapy and spiritual healers. I also recommend more conversations with your mom, potentially addressing these questions and more, if possible. Embrace this question as a pathway to healing some of your guilt while learning more about yourself.

With Love –

XOXO, Lara ♥

BABY?

Should I have a baby? Adopt? Both?

- Monica

Dear Monica,

Oh, my goodness, this is a *big* question. Society says, "Yes, have babies. Raise babies. Be a mother. Have a family."

Should you have a baby, adopt, or both? If you are considering both, I say go for it! As in, if you have the love and space to adopt babies into your life = YES. There are so many babies in the world who need homes. And if you are open to taking on the role of parent, imagine the impact of doing so.

HEAD HEART GUT

Your Head cannot make this decision for you. Head is going to be really great at making pro and con lists, bombarding you with all the reasons *not* to have a baby, and making you really crazy running in circles with these thoughts. Head will always be in the picture, but when it comes to baby-making and baby-having, Head is best suited taking a back seat.

Heart has what you seek. Heart is always loving and looking to expand love. Heart knows that bringing babies and children into your life shows you different forms and ways of loving. Heart is stretching and doing gymnastics and laughing with kids. Heart loves families, the genetic ones and chosen ones. Head will likely be confused and scared when you let Heart lead the way. In my experience, this is how expanding your family sometimes feels - a bit of a tug of war between Head and Heart.

Gut experiences the ocean of emotions that comes alongside a question such as this one. Gut rides the stormy waves of Head's pro and con lists and all the scary things that are involved in having a baby or adopting one. Gut sets sail with eyes on the horizon with Heart at the helm. Gut and Heart together are where the reserves of courage and patience are. Allow Gut to feel all the feelings. It is important to acknowledge the emotional rollercoaster that is involved in scenarios such as this one. Fertility, babies, family and all that go with it are complex. Acknowledge and integrate your feelings and experiences as they come. This decision will be an orchestra of all your senses.

To better understand and tease out what your body may be telling you, here are some questions to journal on:

- What is the pro and con list that Head has come up with?
- What is your Heart's desire in expanding your family?
- What does your Gut tell you when you imagine your life without children?
- When you imagine your life in old age, what do you see?

EXISTENTIAL

All the things! Death! Regret! The meaning of it all! Think about the apocalypse! Or don't. Think about the best version of the world and how your kid is going to contribute to it! Dream great things. Don't dwell on the bad ones. These are the frantic thoughts that run through my brain when I think about having and raising children. I often have my father's voice in my head: "the world is becoming a better and better place!" And it is precisely my family that led me to wanting children.

I always knew that eventually I would want to build my own family. The wanting for family was very clear to me but wanting to be a mom felt less clear. I have often said, "I know that I want kids, the problem is that then you have to raise them." I laugh when I say this, but perhaps I should stop saying it all together. Being a mom is hard and I can't claim that I've ever dreamed of being a *mom*. But somewhere deep inside me, I do long for the closeness and the intimacy that comes alongside raising children. Sometimes I wish I had had the conviction to be a really great Aunt. That was never in the cards, though.

I knew I wanted kids, but I don't love taking care of children for hours on end. Especially in the middle of the night. I hate not sleeping. I hate the intense insomnia I have developed. I loathe the resulting depression I struggle with because I am so sleep deprived.

I am sharing this to illustrate the complexities of deciding to have kids. Yes, things are different when kids are yours because you are the primary. You have to make all the decisions. Even legally, you are required to do that. Not because you are exceptionally awesome or particularly qualified (quite the opposite, remember, anyone can have a kid) - you are the legal guardian of your child, so suddenly you have to think about your own life, decision-making, and your beliefs about things so that you can impose all of it onto your kid.

No one told me how you will have to look so deeply at yourself that you will want to barf and cry all the time when you have kids. I'm not saying it would have changed my decision. I'm saying that maybe we could prepare people better if we did.

On that note, there are many people who absolutely love spending time with kids and raising them. I am so grateful and in awe of those people. You should probably talk to some of them and see what they have to say about deciding to grow your family. Having children is another selfish act, a way of defining our legacies, inflating our own purpose in life, etc.

PROFESSIONAL

There are many good essays and books written about having children, not having children, and passively allowing the child-rearing years to pass. There's one book in particular that comes to mind: *Selfish, Shallow, and Self-absorbed: Sixteen Writers on the Decision to Not Have Kids*, by Meghan Daum.

I mention this one because it is controversial, brash and honest. If you are leaning toward having children, this book will likely give you pause and may even come off as offensive. I think it is important to consider all the aspects of the procreating conundrum. The stories and opinions in Daum's book are rarely considered and are regularly frowned upon. It sheds light on the science behind maternal instincts and the immense pressure on women to have children, regardless of their own desire or any other aspect of individuality. If this sounds like too much, consider other texts that address the issue in more of a pro/con fashion.

You can actively make this decision or passively make this decision. I recommend actively. Schedule time to discuss the decision to have children with your partner if you have one. Google articles on topics to talk about before having kids. What are the obstacles to deciding whether or not to have kids? How might you overcome them and come to greater clarity?

Make an appointment with your doctor and get their professional opinion. It may end up that it isn't a decision you get to make at all. Therefore, by gathering all the information you can, you will reveal more about the reality at hand, including your feelings about all of it.

Having children is very stressful, and they change everything. They change your life in ways you can never imagine or plan for. Therefore, no amount of planning and imagining will really prepare you for having kids. That's not to deter the planning and visioning, do those things too. However, contemplating your life 10, 20, 30 years down the road and beyond can illuminate potential regrets. What do you want your life in old age to be like? How might you feel at sixty plus? Will you regret never having children?

Death and regret often present us with questions regarding legacy. You can use death and regret as tools to build a values compass. Understanding your values and what kind of legacy you want to leave behind is often very clarifying.

In nature, without intervention, children eventually happen. It is so great to not have that be our autopilot. We have choices! Consider the following:

- What is your relationship to your autonomy?

- What role does your partner play in making this decision?

- When you think about nap schedules, not sleeping yourself, and eighteen years of responsibility (minimum), what comes up for you?

- What is your experience with children thus far?

Raising a kid is an around the clock job for a long, long, *long* time. Knowing what you like and what you dislike about raising humans is good because then you can outsource some of the stuff that you don't like as much. If you have the means, get as much help as you can accept. With real community comes support. For those of us living in modern America, in which community is sparse, sometimes you have to pay for support systems.

People do not and almost *can't* give you the truth about what raising kids is like. For example, I couldn't really imagine or believe the poop stories I heard about babies. Now that I have had two kids, I know what it's like to end up with infant poop all over the wall, find it in my hair, and even the dog's mouth before I could do anything to prevent the incident. Also consider the cruelty of toddlers. I still never quite expected the intense volume of my four-year-old shrieking because she wanted Paw Patrol over Sesame Street. Or getting bitten in the back of my thigh by my two-year-old for not being able to correctly build the bed they want on the living room floor.

Go babysit. Take a friend's kid every day after school. Or watch them for a full week while the parents go away (Whoa, you would be a saint!)

If you have one kid, assuming you have a healthy, average kid, it is a lot less hard than two. I say that after having had two in eighteen months. So, what I mean to say is that when you have one kid and just one kid, you go through all the things only once: the stages, the growth, and the changes. But once the kid does stuff for themselves, things become a bit easier again. If you do not have a second child, you can return to a slightly more normal working adult life sooner, if that's what you want.

The problem is that you never know what kind of kid you are going to get. My kids happen to be terrible sleepers and therefore terrible travelers. You can have a colicky baby that screams all the time, you can have sick kids, or you could also have one that down the road you simply do not click with. Again, people rarely speak of these things in public. Even from my mother, I feel like I got romanticized rainbow cereal stories. Parenting is by far the most difficult and taxing thing I have ever done in my life. And while I love my children dearly, the early stages haven't been a walk in the park for me. Postpartum depression, which is alive and well, is another issue that many would rather ignore.

Look, we can do hard things. People have kids all the time. There are lots of options for having kids and how to raise them. Having kids is hard with unforeseen issues every step of the way.

Statistically, most people have children. It's socially unacceptable to say that you regret having kids, so of all the things I have mentioned, that is the one you will probably find the least amount of evidence for. You will probably have at least one kid. You will love that kid. You will learn so much about yourself, your partner, and the world through your kid. It is one wild adventure every single time a new kid comes into existence.

The day-to-day act of raising a human is an act of love. However, it's essential to recognize that it is often not fun and is a 24 hour a day, 365 days a year job. Even though I knew it before having kids, I didn't *get it*. Like *feel* it in my body or have any clue of what this actually means.

American culture does not celebrate childcare or any other form of care. It is unseen and unpaid work. And when someone pays for it, it's likely to be an insultingly low paycheck. The double-standard of being a working mom while also being an at-home mom who spends a lot of time with her kid is alive and well. I intentionally write mom here and am writing in a binary perspective because, in my experience and my learning, people who are embracing the gender spectrum or who are in LGBTQIA+ relationships are more intentional and deliberate in their house and child-rearing roles.

Despite being incredibly expensive, America underpays childcare. Caregiving roles rarely include benefits. Americans still lack basic healthcare around pregnancy, birth, and raising a child. Americans also, for the most part, get little to no maternity/paternity/family leave to care for their families, let alone paid leave. The research is out there, and I encourage you to find it - having kids in this country is punished again and again, at every turn.

I am passionate about these topics: childcare, education, healthcare, community, and being an ambitious woman. I have two little mixed-race girls and I am fighting for a better future for them. Consider the issues you will have to confront as a parent. Also consider the issues your children will have to deal with because they aren't asking to be brought into this world just to satisfy you. From the moment they are born, they become fully formed humans with very real personalities and preferences.

Make an active, informed decision. Know that regretting parts of it and feeling miserable throughout the process is totally normal. Hire a therapist, recruit a coach, and find friends who will support you through the ups and downs of this process.

With love, strength, & vigor –

xoxo,

LARA

SOMEONE ELSE'S DREAM

To what extent should I adjust my dreams to fit and support the dream-accomplishing timeline of someone I love?

-DAB

Dear DAB,

Your question strikes right into my heart. I feel that this has been a repeated theme in my life, and not in an easy, romantic sense, but in a fraught, heartbreaking way. I will attempt to be as unbiased as possible in my response.

HEAD HEART GUT

Head has a lot of opinions about this, but despite all of its knowledge, it may still feel confused and stuck. Head weighs the pros and cons, making all kinds of lists, as though writing down all the possible thoughts and ideas will somehow unravel the right answer. Head wants to have all the things at once. Head wants to crack this code and *win*! Head has a hard time falling asleep at night, mulling over the various possibilities and scenarios to this question.

Heart yearns for a fair answer that accommodates both sides where no one needs to compromise. Heart is striving for a triple win. Heart wants things to be fair and equitable. Heart wants to shower loved ones with support while maintaining its self-compassion and boundaries. Heart can hold all these ideas at once, but reality does not always accommodate them.

Gut is feeling the compromise and is borrowing plenty of worry about what the future holds or what it might be giving up. Sometimes Gut feels sick at the thought of having to set a boundary or at the idea of disappointing people you love. However, Gut also feels hungry for your own dreams and longs to stay true to itself. Gut says, *I'm satisfied when I pursue my truth.*

Unfortunately, you need your Head for making some decisions. I say unfortunately because our heads are super powerful executives, but can often mess us up. Humans are horrible at making decisions, especially happy, healthy ones. Don't believe me? Listen to *The Happiness Lab* podcast with Dr. Laurie Santos.

Heart and Gut are always essential players. The more you can get in touch with them and have them guide you to useful, happy, and healthy decisions, the better. Good luck. This is dependent on who you are, your values, your desires, and what you want to do in your time on earth.

Heart could be misleading here because when Heart is in love, Heart could self-sabotage because it wants to do everything for love. Your Heart is your own personal portal to agape, so loving yourself is very important. Loving is the Heart's true purpose. We are here to love and respect ourselves. Like I said, Heart doesn't want there to have to be compromises. But this is real life, not Heart Amusement Park.

Gut knows the truth. Gut knows the love that Heart feels. Gut knows what this relationship means to them. Gut understands that life doesn't go on forever. Gut gets the idea that you can have it all, just not all at the same time. Gut knows compromise. Gut knows what it can stomach and what it can't. We love to ignore Gut. I don't know why, but humans override their guts constantly. It's called being out of touch with your intuition. It's that quiet voice inside of you that you recognize down the road with *I had a feeling*, or *I knew something wasn't right* --that's Gut barking up your tree (the tree is your spine) yelling at Head saying, *Hello! Please pay attention!*

What do you have to do to be better in touch with your Gut? What's the plan that your mind has already mapped out a million times?

EXISTENTIAL

Existentialism asks us to give things meaning. That can be hard. What does this situation mean to you and your life? What kind of story do you want to tell about this time in the next decade or so? You are going to have to take some action to get more information. Taking no action or making no decisions is also a choice. I believe you are creative and ambitious. There are strange and wonderful solutions in continuing to work on your dreams. It just might not be how you thought.

Have you read Michele Obama's book *Becoming*? It is incredible to learn about the First Lady's relationship with her husband, president Barack Obama. She did not want to be in the public eye and did not like that her husband was so absent when they had young children. She originally wasn't interested in raising their family in the White House. Michele Obama has been on a long journey with herself and her family in these intense transitions. I love that she speaks and writes about it so openly.

I relate so much to her journey. I am married to a doctor and, similar to the presidency, doctors work rule their lives. The training and lifestyles are very demanding. In vocations where there is little wiggle room regarding scheduling, you must be cutthroat in your boundaries and clear in your values. You have to figure out how to make it work.

PROFESSIONAL

Since I don't have any details of your situation to go on, I'm going to do a big dump of decision-making tools I use and recommend:

- Use the Bento Box decision-making tool from bentoism. org.
- Do at least three Odyssey Plans from *Designing Your Life*.
- Have the person you love do Odyssey plans.
- Reflect on your past regrets: what can you learn from them? (see the Transforming Regrets worksheet in the free downloadable workbook).
- Talk about flexibility and timing with your partner. What options are available to you?
- Make a list of wishes you have for the future. Discuss them with this person.
- Journal on the following questions:
    - What would it take to feel good about bending to your partner's timeline?
    - What would feel good about sticking to your own timeline?
    - Is there any overlap?

- Write yourself a letter: three years have passed, and you are feeling great about your decisions. What has transpired?

- Are there any crazy options that you haven't considered yet?

- Talk to your family and friends to review your thinking and any progress you make using these tools to find answers.

- Finally, check out *The Decision Book: 50 Models for Strategic Thinking* by Mikeal Krogerus and Roman Tschäppeler

Action leads to clarity. Clarity leads to confidence. With each decision you make, you will need to act, and those actions are all votes in favor of the direction you are choosing to go. Said differently, making no decision is passively choosing to continue down the road you're now on. It sounds like there is some kind of an insurmountable problem that requires sacrifice. Define what the real problems are so that you can begin exploring potential solutions.

For example, if your partner has received an acceptance to medical school in Denver, the problem may arise from the fact that you are pursuing a career in San Francisco. If you want to be in the same location, you will be required to move, as it is unlikely that your partner is going to give up their medical journey. However, if you are both open to exploring a long-distance relationship, then a bunch of alternative arrangements open up. This is a gross simplification, but an example straight out of my life that feels relevant every day.

Create a spreadsheet of the various categories of problems you can identify: location, finances, career, responsibilities, etc. Where can you find wiggle room? Hire a coach, do some therapy, and carve out the time to genuinely reflect on your situation. There are many ways to support the dreams of the people you love. The question here is one of sacrifice.

Where there's a will, there's a way - I believe that. Your dreams will change, and you will make edits to your approach, but you may not need to abandon your plans. If there are edits you are upset by and you are required to sacrifice your own dreams for now, perhaps there is a spiritual journey that is seeking you. What is the transformation that is looking to happen in your life?

In solidarity –

STAY OR GO

Should I stay or should I go?

Dear Stay or Go,

My off-the-cuff answer is to go. Go take a break. Answers and decisions are not written in stone. Action leads to clarity. Clarity leads to more decisions. Decisions and more action lead to confidence. And by confidence, I mean information, definitive answers, a shifting in the situation, and a *greater understanding of where you stand*.

HEAD HEART GUT

Head is gonna beat this one to death. But there's nothing like a solid pro and con list! So do that! I even have one for you in the downloadable workbook.

Heart doesn't want to compromise; it wants it all! It wants to stay and go.

Gut is your internal compass, so pay special attention to it on this journey. Gut is your second brain and has a better understanding of your subconscious than Head does. Do some meditation exercises and see what Gut is telling you.

EXISTENTIAL

The existentialists ask you to define the meaning of staying and going. Then you must decide for yourself how to move forward with integrity.

PROFESSIONAL

I recommend the Bento Box decision-making matrix to consider *future you* and *future us*. I also recommend reading *The Power of Regret* by Dan Pink. Get together your most trusted advisers and discuss the situation with them. A note of caution: asking for advice can be challenging and potentially harmful, depending on the details of the situation. However, if your advisers know you intimately and care about you, they can support you in making a good decision.

If you need an immediate course of action, choose one and see how it works out for you for a limited time. Then prototype the other one! You've painted a black-and-white picture, but as your coach I'm required to challenge you: What shades of gray might you consider? You can never truly reverse a decision, you must move forward from where you are.

Choose boldly,

Lara ♡

P.S. There are worksheets waiting for you in the workbook to help you make your bold decision! Check out the Bold Choice Worksheet among others.

SOCIAL BUTTERFLY

Dear Lara,

Riddle me this: I'm a social butterfly who almost everyone in my life sees as an extrovert but am actually a hair over the line on the introvert side. I have been feeling the need to slow down in my life, but I don't know how. I have many friends in Denver and around the world who I don't see or talk to as much as I'd like, as well as lots of activities I adore (hiking/biking/rock climbing/museums/etc.). I'd love any advice you have on how to be more intentional about my social schedule in a way that includes nurturing my inner introvert.

-Tes

Dear Tes,

I know 100% of what you are talking about. I, too, am a social butterfly, a hair over the line toward introvert. When I met you and experienced your exuberant energy, you were standing in front of a packed room on an open mic. I marveled at your alive-ness and your involvement in many meaningful projects.

You seem like a complete powerhouse, ready to take on the world. You don't shy away from conversation; you invite it all in.

You have a self-imposed scheduling problem and an energy distribution problem. So, let's get down to the brass tacks.

HEAD HEART GUT

Head knows that extroverts get rewarded in society. Head also knows that it can feel great to be *out there* socializing and doing everything. There are lots of dopamine hits with extroverted activities, which can be exciting. Head loves the thinking break it gets from being present with friends.

However, when Head has spent all its energy and needs to be recharged, things can go a little haywire. For Head, this probably looks like going from present to zoning out, being energized to feeling drained, and perhaps getting irritable. Head is going to be useful in solving the scheduling puzzle, though it is going to need a hand from Heart and Gut to really follow through. More on that in a moment.

Heart also loves the delicious satisfaction of being in the presence of good company. Heart feels full when relationships are nourished. However, Heart can feel heavy when its needs for rest and quiet aren't honored. That may look like feeling sad in a joyful situation or even missing yourself.

Gut loves the rollercoaster ride it experiences with the excitement and energy of social interaction. However, Gut might be the first to tell you, *that's enough.* I'm sensing a lot of Gut in the wording of your question. You ask how to *be more intentional* with your schedule to *nurture your inner introvert*, which illustrates that Gut has brought it to your attention and that it needs to be honored and included in this process.

Let Heart and Gut lead the way in your scheduling conundrum. Head is going to do its thing, working the calendar like a 1000-piece puzzle. What would Heart and Gut say if they could speak? Perhaps it's more one-on-one hangouts in nature or simply finding small, intentional moments of quiet in between events.

EXISTENTIAL

We are all going to die someday. In learning about death and regret, most often people regret things they did not do rather than things they did. This is a context-dependent statement, but it works here in relation to your question.

Many people prefer to keep a busy social calendar because of the fear of missing out (FOMO). And this makes sense with social media and being so in touch with each other these days. In the *Designing Your Life* (DYL) coaching world, we have another acronym: JOMO.

JOMO is the *joy of missing out*. It is the ownership associated with making a conscientious choice, an intentional slowing down, and being at peace with the fact that we cannot do or be everything at once.

This puts us at a crossroads.

Do you continue to pursue your current level of activity because you might regret it if you don't? Do you embrace a busy social life to avoid missing out? People who socialize a lot tend to be quite happy and have a lot of life experiences out there in the world with others.

Consider the alternative with these questions:

- How can you monitor your energy levels and find a way of embracing JOMO?
- What quality of interactions do you want to have?
- What's the price of constantly making yourself available to others?

- Is there something missing from your life puzzle that you might regret if you did not honor it more during your time here?

- And finally, what would *future you* thank your *present you* for?

PERSONAL EXPERIENCE

Your question strikes close to my heart because many folks would describe me as an extrovert. Little do they know that I happily work solo, whether in an art studio or a private home office. I can write, draw, read, and have 1:1's with clients all day. My alone time is extremely precious to me, and unless I have deeply nourishing connections with people, I am quickly drained of energy in a social setting.

If I don't get my solo time in, I have problems. I wear my feelings on my sleeve, and I get very short with the people around me. When I am rested, I am a goddamn fucking ray of sunshine. When I'm pooped, I'll likely bite your head off (those close to me know what I'm talking about). I'm like Pepa Madrigal from the Disney film *Encanto*. You can see the storm clouds forming over my head when shit is bad.

My work in the world is deeply connected to the time I have for reflection. That happens through my writing and my art. Coaching is a dream profession for me because it gives me a huge dose of the interactions I absolutely love to have with folks: deep, meaningful conversations about super real shit.

Art is another important practice for me, and one that also connects me to a community and creates interesting dialogue. I love a good party, dancing at concerts, and I've taught myself how to strike up conversations with strangers. That doesn't change my introverted-ness. It simply means that I've developed some mad skills when it comes to talking to people and creating the life that I want to live.

Having spent time with you, I know you have some of these skills yourself. There's no doubt in my mind that you can create the balance you seek. Perhaps it's a seasonal thing. Sun's out, it's time to party. Winter temps? Hello, hibernation. I'm excited to hear what you come up with.

PROFESSIONAL

We can start at a surface level and dig deeper as we go. Your scheduling problem, though potentially exhausting, is both solvable and manageable in various ways.

There is a well-known story about a university professor who illustrated prioritizing our time using a jar, rocks, pebbles, sand, and water. Many YouTube videos show his illustration. If you put the rocks in first, then the pebbles, then the sand, and finally the water, it all fits. This exercise illustrates the importance of making space for your biggest and most important priorities. Everything else can fit around those.

A practical approach to your question is to schedule time for yourself and activities you want to accomplish alone. Every once in a while, when I have a break in my schedule, I like to spontaneously treat myself to some self-care. Perhaps that is more your style. Is there an hour's break where you can lie in bed and read a book? Soak in a tub for 20 minutes?

Take the time to review your calendar. What are your big rocks? If you notice that you have something planned every night of the week, specifically carve out a solo evening. Tell people you have a work project or a meeting if you have to. Or just say, "I already have plans," or "I have a date" ☺.

I would like you to sit down and journal on the following questions:

- How does indulging in an active social life benefit you?
- In what ways is a busy calendar hindering you?
- What will it take to accept the situation as is?
- What will it take to make the desired changes in your schedule?

Without the answers to these questions, you will likely only take time to yourself when you are completely burned out on socializing. Is that a system that works for you? Because if it does, that" ok, too. What is your soul craving? What is the crux of needing to make any sort of intentional change? Unlocking that truth for yourself will set you free.

From one extroverted introvert to another,

LOVE LIFE

What can I do to get my love life going again?

Love, Albert

Dear Albert,

When I read your question, I'm reminded of my own recommitment to dating and love back in 2014. I was living in San Francisco which, for several reasons, can be a very challenging city to find a long-term partner in. Dating is no problem. There are lots of men, but little commitment. So, I dated *a lot*. It was exhilarating, frustrating, mysterious, and adventurous.

One adventure included dropping off my date at a bus station in the Richmond district late at night after a horrible dinner, listening to him name dropping and bragging about his accomplishments. He was a terrible conversation partner, to say the least.

Another escapade included a hotel manager with a New York accent, who I thought was a booty-call until he asked me to meet his mom. What even happened there?! (Sorry Joe!)

Yet another relationship was a boyfriend I met surfing in Costa Rica who lived in Atlanta, Georgia. He was a firefighter and very good looking. Unfortunately, he ghosted for weeks after joining me on a trip to Mexico with close friends.

And finally, no San Franciscan dating repertoire is complete without the Burning Man relationship. That turned out to be an absolutely horrible match, something I couldn't admit until the dust had literally settled.

When I had enough of the ups and downs on my search for sex, fun, adventure, lovers, and ultimately a good friend and life partner, I resorted to buying a book that surpassed my comfort level of woo. That book is called *Calling in the One* by Katherine Woodward Thomas. Or maybe it's just the title that makes me feel embarrassed. Either way, I read the book and, as far as I can remember, did the exercises. I don't know how much time elapsed, but I ended up meeting my future husband around the same time.

It wasn't obvious that we would build a long-lasting relationship. It was the opposite. I resisted the relationship with my now husband with a great deal of effort. I probably never would have agreed to be in a committed relationship with him if my mom hadn't brought him up after an event I hosted, asking "*Who is that man?*" He had specifically sought out and bought my mom a drink, charming her in whatever small talk conversation ensued. My husband can be a very charming man.

If you're struggling with commitment, I can relate. It took eight to nine months for me to finally fully commit to a real partnership with Adrian (my partner). During that time, Adrian and I agreed to be together, as in exclusively date. I had been his boss for a year at the small gym I managed and he was moving back to Southern California for a new job. A week after we started dating, he moved to Long Beach, and we began a long-distance relationship. I figured our time together would find a natural conclusion. Adrian had other plans, and so did I. While Adrian put his best foot forward, calling, texting, visiting, and showering me with devotion - I was busy planning a surf-bicycle trip that would take me to

Sydney, Australia. Six months after we started dating, I bought a one-way ticket to the land down under.

It was during this adventurous, wild, and lonely trip in Australia that my commitment to Adrian solidified. I believe that all the work that I did with the book *Calling in the One* began to coalesce in a way that I could understand. I struggled to accept love when it was readily given to me, particularly when it was showered on me enthusiastically. To me, it proved that there was something wrong with the other person. I knew that putting some of my own bullshit aside would not be enough to make the relationship between Adrian and me work. However, I would have to give it an honest chance, a real effort, to see if it was even possible.

Are we a good match? So far, going on nine years together, I can say honestly, we are.

Several serendipitous events played into sparking my love life. What my mom saw in Adrian on the evening of the art reception and reading *Calling in the One* meant something. I know that we must make space for the things we really want in our lives. Even when something wonderful falls in our lap, over time, you need to nurture and respect that thing for it to flourish.

This gives you some background about my own dating trials and tribulations. For a while, I considered becoming a dating or relationship coach. So, thank you, Albert, for giving me the opportunity to share about love and dating here.

HEAD HEART GUT

Head is always jabbering on saying, *I know what to do*. Head loves knowing all the answers. Head will often give you answers even when it is primarily fluff to satisfy a curious and frightened mind. This looks like Head coming up with long to do lists about how it could get your love life started again. It also looks like a long list of reasons you should not get started on the to do list just yet. Head may tell you stories explaining your particular situation for hours into the night because Head likes to have stories that make sense of things. Head likes to keep you safe and will rationalize each step of your journey. This could be a direct result of lived experiences, such as break up's, abandonment, and attachment issues.

Head can also be on your side by feeding you creative actions and championing you along the way. Signed up for a dating app? *Good job*! Asked your friend to set you up on a blind date? *High five*! Whichever side Head is on for you at the moment, keep your chin up and tune into Heart and Gut.

Heart says, *let us love more again*. Heart always wants to expand love, every expression of it. Heart wants to share love and grow it in the process. Heart knows that any expression of love is an act of growing and expanding. Darryl Anka said, "Everything is energy and that's all there is to it. Match the frequency of the reality you want and you cannot help but get that reality. It can be no other way. This is not philosophy. This is physics." Which is to say that love begets love. Heart knows and lives the energy frequency of love every day. It is always there for you and is ready to be channeled toward your desires.

Gut may be feeling nervous. Gut will be your ally in knowing the love that feels good to you. Put another way, Gut is your love compass. Pay attention to the signals your body gives you as you get to know new people. What type of compatibility are you looking for? How does this person fit into your life? Gut will provide clearer answers than Head. Gut will calibrate over time and deepen your understanding of what exactly it is you are looking for. Gut knows that there are different types of love and all of them increase the capacity for Head, Heart and Gut to function together. Love is an energy generating frequency. Gut senses this when it is experiencing it. Gut says, *hold on tight! We will do this together!*

EXISTENTIAL

Even though the majority of us will interpret love life as romantic love, I would like to take a moment here to explore the depth and breadth of love. Western culture puts pressure on modern relationships to be at the level of soul mate. That one person in the world who can and should fulfill all your needs: emotional, physical, sexual, intellectual, etc. We are complex human beings that have a lot of needs. Humans are needy. It is unrealistic that one person could meet all our needs all the time.

Love life could simply mean exploring love and growing our capacity for it in all its different forms: the love we have for our friends, our children, our pets, or even the love of an activity or place. I imagine that you, Albert, have had an active loving relationship at some point, perhaps with parents, siblings, and even children.

I personally come from a large, tight-knit family. My relationships with my siblings have shown me how profound and dedicated familial connections can be. They have also helped me make distinctions in my chosen family and friendships. In light of the different relationships that we have experienced during our lifetime, chosen family and friends teach us important things about love.

My siblings, for example, continue to be one of the most important support structures in my life. We have so much shared history, which makes for ease of context and an understanding around belief systems, values, and desires. I have two sisters and a brother. They have seen me throughout so many transitions. They often remind me of my childhood dreams, help me see myself in a new light, and offer a sympathetic ear during hard times. They also continue to show me how important it is to have relationships in my life where open and honest communication happens. That includes arguing, giving space, and repairing. This is a level of priceless intimacy, knowing that someone loves you at your best and will continue to love you during your worst.

In the same way that humans need different types of rest, we also need different types of love. You need familial love (immediate family or chosen family), you need community and friends, and you need self-love. Knowing that men often have a difficult time making friends and maintaining friendships, you might find this *New York Times* article useful. I want to encourage you to look at all the things you have learned from folks about love.

Journal about the following questions to uncover some of what you have learned over your lifetime:

- What have all of your different relationships taught you?

- How could you explore your love life by nurturing these different forms of love?

- If love is energy and energy seeks like energy, how can you love yourself today?

- And, if it feels right, who else can you express love toward today?

Remember, this is a vulnerable journey you are embarking on. It can't be overstated how important it is to be open, kind, and patient with yourself. It is surprising how much easier it can be to express love or kindness toward someone else but deny it to yourself. Having clarity around the type of love you need and want to increase in your life right now will help you build a clear and actionable plan to move forward with. Take the time to do some self-reflection and some dreaming around what you truly seek.

Love can come as a text message, a letter, a hug, a phone call. Love is a listening ear. Love is remembering a birthday. Love is a spontaneous compliment. Love is shared laughter. Love is going out of your way to support someone. I believe that if you engage in these forms of loving actions, your approach to the specific love life you seek will expand exponentially faster than otherwise.

PROFESSIONAL

Congratulations Albert! You are ready to embark on an exhilarating journey! The love life path is always full of trials, tribulations, and wild tales.

The good news is that there are so many wonderful ways to get your love life going again! Hiring a dating coach is one of them. There are also dozens of great dating apps that make getting into the dating world easy. From dating specific to more casual recommendations, you could join an interest group, a hobby club, or a neighborhood sports league. You could also start attending networking events; dating specific ones would be the most fruitful. There are even travel agencies that set up group travel for singles!

The pros of investing in various dating services are that you are significantly more likely to get your love life going again on a shorter timeline. It can be a serious challenge for some to get back into the dating world. Meeting new dating partners in the real world can be preferred and sound nice, but it can also pose a significant challenge - we may encounter people who are not seeking the same thing, are already in relationships, or have different priorities. Vetting the pool of potential dating candidates can increase your success. The cons are that it's scary to get involved in online dating because of the level of mystery behind each person. Cons range from the long list of unknowns about someone to the time and effort these pursuits take. Decide what your priorities are and how to move forward.

Depending on your style of interacting with others and your interests, it would be best to research what feels good to you. Consider the following questions to get you started on a more specific path:

- Are you introverted or extroverted?

- Would you like a partner who will do certain activities with you? Do you want to find partners with similar interests? Pickleball, the fastest growing sport in America, could be a great way to find a sports partner. A chess club or writing group could introduce you to gaming or creative partners.

- What does getting your love life started again mean to you?

- Do you want to just date for fun or are you looking to be matched with someone who is a potential long-term partner?

If you decide that dating apps, dating, and using dating services are a good option for you: sign up. Don't go it alone, get help! Having friends and confidantes who can help you build a good profile is priceless. How well you are matched with potential partners depends on the quality of your profile. "What's a good profile?" you might ask. This is not my area of expertise and where a dating coach and other app experienced people would be of great use to you. I would say that a good profile is one that is tailored to getting the specific results you are searching for, whether it be casual dating, long-term relationships, or activity partners, etc. Invest in knowledgeable feedback here to accelerate your results.

If you are committed to meeting people in the real world, consider reaching out to friends and trusted individuals to introduce you to potential partners. A friend of mine started a dating project where she asked her entire trusted network to keep her in mind for blind dates. She requested if friends knew someone single ready to date, that they set her up. She aims to go on one date a month at a minimum. I found this idea incredibly creative and a great way for her network to support her.

The beauty of today's world is that there are so many options to tackle your exact question, Albert. Whether it's finding a romantic pen pal or a partner ready to travel abroad, there are great resources waiting for you to explore!

To reiterate, here is my suggested plan for you to start your love life back up:

- Make a list of ways you will put yourself out there.

- List what you are looking for in your next version of your love life.

- List out specifics or non-negotiables if you feel called to do so but keep this list short as allowing this list to get long tends to shut the door on potential good matches before you have even given them a chance.

- If you are open to dating apps, find a friend who can help you build an accurate profile based on the results you are looking for.

- Consider hiring a dating coach if you're looking for a specific relationship or feel that you are struggling with specific blocks to getting your love life going again.

- Research hobby/sport/interest groups in your area where you can meet people in person.

- Talk to your friends (and your greater network depending on your comfort level): tell them you are ready to get your love life going again. Let them know what introductions you are looking for.

- Connect with a friend who can support you along the bumpy road of love life trials.

- Be kind and gentle with yourself.

- Celebrate after each step that you take and every time you put yourself out there!

Best of luck, Albert. I am excited about all the love life adventures that await you!

Love, strength & vigor,

Lara ♥

CAREER

"Success is only meaningful and
enjoyable if it feels like your own."

– Michelle Obama

WHOLE SELF

How do I bring my "whole self" to work, find the right culture and the right job that makes me happy all in one? So, essentially, the meaning of life.

Dear Whole Self,

Your question made me laugh out loud a bit. I love that you wrapped it up as "the meaning of life" because of course, the career world would like to think that it is *everything*. The current culture in America is that career and work are the most important things in life. No matter my feelings around your question, I, too, ask these of myself and my work. It is the precise reason that I keep working at having a location independent business where I get to make (some of) the rules.

However, you are talking about four different things here, all of which are pretty big concepts on their own:

1. Your whole self
2. Finding the right workplace culture
3. Finding the right job
4. The meaning of life

Let us get some perspective around what you are looking for.

HEAD HEART GUT

Head is confused and spinning. It has convinced you that you are living in a world where people bring their entire selves to work. It has also convinced you that this place has an excellent work culture and makes its employees happy. Head drank the *love what you do* Kool-Aid that has taught us *you are your work*, your worth is determined by your paycheck, and you derive your meaning from these two things.

Head drinks this Kool-Aid to fit in with the dominant culture and to survive within our current capitalistic systems. There are many avant-garde thought leaders around an individual's purpose and worth outside the realm of work. Oliver Burkeman, the author of *4,000 Weeks,* and Tricia Hersey of *Rest is Resistance,* are two examples of folks questioning the status quo and reminding us that we are not our work, we are extraordinary beings.

Heart and Gut love the idea of the whole self combined with work culture but are laughing and crying at Head as they snuggle below your lungs. Heart knows and beats the truth of being-ness through your veins every day. Heart understands evolution, lineage, and legacy. Heart contains the limitless possibilities of every human ever. Heart knows that you are not your job title, your paycheck, or any other identity label. Heart is where the truth of your worth and purpose reside. The truth being that you are priceless, limitless, and undefinable.

Gut creates a bridge between Heart and Head. Gut wants a job that you can bring your whole self to, but it is also the sensitive messaging system that tells you in nanoseconds when you have made a social snafu. It's like when you get comfortable at work and then make a joke or do an overshare that lands poorly and then you get a vulnerability hangover. Gut makes notes of these moments and reminds you to share more carefully next time.

Gut is the important mechanism that helps us fit in with the herd, with our tribe. We have evolved as group animals. So even when you can't bring your whole self to work, you find ways to be a version of yourself in order to make money, put food on the table, and maintain relationships. Gut is the one who tells us how much we are willing to tolerate at work: how much acceptance and expression do we require to live a good life?

EXISTENTIALISM

The meaning of life you say? From work? *No, no, no*, my friend. The meaning of life rests purely inside of you, solely for you. Work can be an expression of it, but work cannot give you the meaning of life. Work that is an expression of your meaning can be a beautiful thing.

Is it necessary to bring your whole self to work?

Is it even possible?

There are certain boundaries essential to delineating the whole self, culture, jobs, and work that seems important to maintaining our sanity. Some people feel the need to make a job or career out of being themselves. However, even those typically must edit certain facets - whether parts of them are off brand or too tender to share. Simone Stolzoff does a brilliant job of illustrating this in his book, *Good Enough Job*. When we use language around work that begins to blur important boundaries, we get in trouble. Many workplaces today say things like, "we are like family." This is dangerous because it creates an unhealthy and unstable relationship between employer and employee.

Family values are about love, connection, acceptance, and unconditional support. In a work setting, you have an employer who pays you to perform a job. There are consequences for misbehaving and not delivering on the agreement. The employer sits in a position of privilege and control. The employee is not unconditionally accepted, and that is not what we want when we hire someone for a job.

I have thought a lot about Stolzoff's point about healthy boundaries between work and life. Since having kids, I have hired nannies and babysitters, both for longer term jobs and for a few hours in the afternoon. I am guilty of using the language, "we are welcoming you into our family" and other variations because I would love to find a nanny who seamlessly integrates with our family. I realize now that that puts pressure on me and whoever we hire in unfair ways. I want a babysitter who is going to act professionally, be open to feedback, and take good care of our children and I will fire someone if they don't hold up their end of the deal. I don't actually want them to be part of our family. I also want whoever we hire to be able to advocate for themselves and maintain their own boundaries. So, I now steer clear of this kind of language when navigating work situations.

Our current culture is obsessed with the idea of bringing our whole selves to work, but very few people and places manage to make this a reality in a healthy way. This obsession is misplaced. Yes, it is important to work toward a work culture that accepts diversity, wholeness, authenticity, and more openness. However, there is and will always be tension between personal and professional. And that's OK. It's more than OK, it's necessary.

We do not want to blend every aspect of our lives into one. Contrast is the spice of life. It is how we distinguish our experiences.

Finding a good work culture for you right now is important. Making cultural change a priority for yourself is essential if you want to see systemic change in America. Culture is a notoriously difficult thing to change. Learn about what work culture is, how it's created, how to identify it and how to change it. Incorporate that into future interviews and use it for observing your present occupation.

Finding the *right* job may or may not be the answer to your question. A *New York Times* article, *How to Feel Happier at Work When You Have the Urge to Quit,* explores how to change your current work circumstances if quitting isn't the best option. There are small but potent tweaks you can make to your situation that may lead to big changes. The article also points out that we need to consider short-term changes versus long-term ones. Consider your values around work. How might you take a bird's-eye view of your life and see your current situation as a valuable steppingstone?

Another valuable perspective on your queries is looking into Sparketypes. Having recently listened to an episode of the Sparketype Podcast where a doctor is planning to leave her career, the advice given by the Sparked Brain Trust is to slow down, edit the current situation in whatever ways possible, and then to prototype additional redesigns. Listening to this episode with the physician's dilemma, made me think of you, Whole Self.

In your question about finding a job that makes you happy and in the discussion about the doctor's burnout, there's a lot of talk around how so many of us are unhappy in our work. There are potential edits you can make in your current position to make it more fulfilling. A helpful reframe might be: Work isn't intended to make me happy. I am responsible for my happiness. My level of happiness and the things that make me happy will be a compass for knowing if my current work culture is headed in the right direction. For example, overworked people tend to lean toward burnout, which leads to being unhappy. Burned out people don't have time for important things like family, exercise, getting good rest, and hobbies. Build your personal values compass and heed it.

That means not throwing the baby out with the bath water, not quitting from a point of desperation and burnout. Rather, create some space for yourself to really consider all the options available to you and take the time to learn the realities of what values you are living.

It is not your work's responsibility to make you happy, nor will your employer prioritize your happiness. Our current culture around work and the capitalist systems we live within have nothing to do with happiness or purpose. They have to do with the economy, competition, and money. You must define purpose and happiness for yourself. You must find and define the activities and ways of being that make you happy and then diligently implement them into your life.

It is worth mentioning here that doing this can be extremely difficult. Oliver Burkeman's book *4,000 Weeks: Time Management for Mortals* explores how humans are deeply intertwined. He illustrates how individual pursuits deviate and deny our communal nature and interconnectedness. Burkeman does this by highlighting a study in which there was a direct relationship between the amount of people who had time off together and the use of antidepressants. When we can enjoy leisure time together, the collective happiness increases, both in employees' well-being and that of the unemployed or retired.

While we are all unique individuals, we are also part of humanity as a whole and that matters. This is important because this is where many people derive happiness, meaning, and purpose both in their work and personal lives. You have got to define the meaning of life for yourself. I would advise against looking to work to provide this for you. Defining the meaning of life is the perfect work to do with a life or career coach. Define your terms. Make discernments. Get clear on the purpose of work. Understand what you believe about why you are here. Paint your vision.

What's the meaning of your life today?

What do you want it to be twenty years from now?

These aren't rhetorical questions. Answer them and answer them well.

PROFESSIONAL

In this section, we will dissect the different parts of your question in more detail.

1. How do you define your "whole self"? Because if Heart and Gut have anything to do with it, that may mean being able to cry openly at work, have an attitude like you do with a family member, and potentially leave your dishes in the sink. From a professional coach viewpoint, a respectable workplace culture includes cleaning up after yourself, appropriate workplace humor, being on time, and more.

2. How to find the right workplace culture? YES! This is exciting! What does this mean to you? What would a good culture look like and feel like? Write it down!

3. How might one find the right job? Similarly to the workplace culture, become a detective of what the right job is. What do you do now? What would you rather be doing? Don't know? OK, start getting some ideas down on paper and exploring how you might try them on for size.

4. Finally, we have the meaning of life. This is an important one. If finding and defining the meaning of life sounds desirable to you, I encourage you to do this for yourself if you have not already.

Antiquated as it is, classic professionalism is still king around the world. Your homework is to read the *Designing Your Life* book and do all the exercises. Next, please listen to The Happiness Lab episode with Simone Stolzoff about his book, *Good Enough Job*.

It sounds like what you are searching for is a work culture that respects who you are and respects individual expression. Your job does not need to fill all the buckets of your life. The same way that a life partner cannot fulfill all the roles of various relationships in one. Defining your terms will take you far, Whole Self!

Whole heartedly –

xoxo,
Lara

60'S+ SEEKER

I'm in my sixties and need to work for another ten years. Recently I relocated from an urban to a rural area (wondrous!) The small boutique nonprofit I've worked with for twenty years is likely to wind down operations in another eighteen to twenty-four months. CROSSROADS MOMENT: do I look to stay in the same field (needing a remote job that doesn't require a move) or do I look for a more radical reinvention?

Is a second career possible?

Dear 60s+ Seeker,

Congratulations on your wondrous move to the country! It sounds truly lovely and as though it is breathing freshness into your existence. This move illustrates your adventurous nature and the ability to reinvent yourself, regardless of age.

It is precisely these moments of transition that open the door to even greater change. It makes sense you are asking these questions now.

HEAD HEART GUT

Head has you questioning if a second career is possible. Head is excellent at coming up with a list of doubts. Head wants us to be safe and to stay in our lane.

Heart is clearly gleeful with your recent move. That is the sense I get when I read "wondrous!" That is your Heart talking. Heart loves reinvention. Heart loves embracing a beginner's mind. That's the wondrous-ness in so many things. Perhaps this move is a way of showing you that transformation is always possible if that is what you desire. From the phrasing in your question, your Heart is saying, *I'm ready for anything!*

Gut may be sending you mixed messages between Heart and Head. It would only make sense to be nervous about switching industries in your career after being with one organization for so long. But being nervous does not mean don't do it. Your Gut appears to be on board with your recent change from urban to rural.

Gut can get confused about excitement versus anxiety. Fear often shows up in our Gut as anxiety and nervousness. But that is also how excitement shows up for Gut, too. I encourage you to sit down and dig into what Heart and Gut are telling you.

What does your Heart and Gut say about working for another ten years? When you consider a radical career switch, what do your senses tell you? Your body knows things that Head may not be clear on yet. Take some time to digest these questions, as well as some of your own.

EXISTENTIAL

Regret research tells us that living the #noregrets lifestyle is bullshit. When we name and examine our regrets, we have the opportunity to learn something meaningful about ourselves and make better decisions in the future. The time to mine your regrets could be now. If you are waffling between *should I* or *shouldn't I* – asking yourself, *will I regret it if...* could be a powerful reflection. It could be the key to going one way or the other.

This is a good time to take a step back and consider what your work means to you from the perspective of a life span. What significance do you give to your work? What does your work mean to you after all this time? I ask these questions because there can be gold nuggets in your responses. When we take more of a bird's-eye view of our lives and our work, we often find common threads and driving factors that perhaps were not so obvious from the current situation level.

I hope you will have insights here that will make this decision easier and clearer for you. For example:

- Would you regret not switching career tracks now?
- What have you regretted thus far in your life?
- What can you learn from those regrets?
- Is there work you feel you still *have* to do?
- Is there a project, action, or cause that you are extremely passionate about?
- Are there ways that you have been unable to express yourself thus far that are calling to you now?

Work does not need to be all things. Work can pay the bills and support our artistic hobbies. We can fund our travel dreams or build our creative ideas into existence on the side. Of course, you may just be bored with your current situation. In which case, there are a million ways to spice up a career that has gone stale. The question then is do we have the patience to do the work?

Even though I say in the professional section to get a bunch of clarity, clarity can be overrated when you truly are unsure. *You can't think your way through this situation.* It is action that creates clarity and shows you what viable paths forward are. And given that we are working with defined finite stretches of time, you do not have forever to figure out what road to go down. You need to act sooner rather than later.

If you want to give a new industry a go, then see how you can dip your toes into an area that interests you as soon as possible. In the *Designing Your Life* book, they call this prototyping. Create a way to experiment and try a new industry on for size (see the prototyping worksheet in the downloadable workbook). One way of doing this is to have constructive informational interviews with folks, as mentioned in the networking section below.

Alternatively, continuing the work you have no doubt become good at and expanding your horizons in other ways (like moving to a rural area) also seems fulfilling. You can use your expertise to build the life of your dreams outside of work, while perhaps negotiating the flexibility to accommodate it.

PROFESSIONAL

As with any situation, it depends. Let's tease out a few specifics.

Financial Risk Tolerance

Your question of whether to stay in your current position or leave depends on your financial situation and risk tolerance. If you have the desire and the financial means to change industries at this point in your career with another decade to go, I would say go for it. The nonprofit world is not going anywhere. Part-time work could bridge the gap between what you do now and where you want to go. This could be the biggest factor in your decision. If you need new training or to make new connections to land your desired position in a new industry, do you have the financial means to do so?

If, at the moment, it is too risky to leave, my professional opinion is to stay in your current position until they shut down or your transition plan is in place. It is the stable situation that will give you more freedom and flexibility to explore what comes next. The stability of your current position will help with planning your next steps regardless of the direction you decide to go.

Switching Industries & Reinvention

Take the time to review the pros and cons of staying in your current industry. Download the Workbook and fill out the Pro's & Con's Worksheet. Do a search for positions you might apply for to see what is available. Reflect on these questions and see what answers you come up with.

- What leads you to consider switching industries?
- What feels exciting about doing something totally new?
- What are legitimate obstacles or reasons for staying in the same field?

Radical reinvention is possible! Reinventions aren't easy. That does not mean they aren't fun. Transformations are sexy and alluring! Many of us love the idea of a big transformation, but the reality is that they are often unsettling and rocky for a period of time.

Start by understanding your desire for radical reinvention. As you uncover both your dreams and professional desires, start having conversations with people about the potential options you are considering. Leveraging your network and doing informational interviews are essential in creating your path forward.

Professionally speaking, I suggest starting out by understanding your motivations for a significant change. If it is happiness or simplicity of lifestyle that you seek, then that should play a role in your decision-making. Happiness research says we are happier when we are sufficient and good at what we do. That usually comes with time and experience. So, depending on your motivations, it could benefit you to stay in your current field and have that work support additional learning or training to freshen things up or even get you started in a new direction.

If, like me, you love reflecting, I recommend creating a container time period in which to wrap up your reflection work. Time feels of the essence here and we want to create forward movement. Which brings me to networking - talking and collaborating your way to reinvention.

Networking

In my coaching business, I like to use the term *leveraging your network*. I say this to illustrate that we need to be pulling the strings in our community web and connecting with our people regularly to make networking magic happen. When we are in community and in conversation, wonderful opportunities present themselves. Plus, research has shown that having lots of conversations with various types of people throughout the day significantly increases our happiness—a bonus to networking in all its forms!

I imagine that the organization you are currently with has a robust network. Both internal (like other employees and leaders) and external (other organizations it is connected to, conferences, etc.). How might your company aid you in moving on? Who do your coworkers know? What other organizations are tied to yours? Who have you worked with over your time there who you can reconnect with?

Take the time to schedule coffee dates with acquaintances. One this week, two the next. Make a habit of connecting with people actively moving forward. This is a way to make sure you are in the right place at the right time for additional introductions or opportunities to present themselves. By that, I mean you never know who you will get connected to or what opportunities you may stumble across.

Your homework is to start having conversations with people!

Whatever choices you make moving forward, 60s+ Seeker, you seem ready for life's adventures. I believe you will make the best out of whatever you decide.

With love, strength & vigor –

LARA

are tied to yours? Who have you worked with over your time there who you can reconnect with?

Take the time to schedule coffee dates with acquaintances. One this week, two the next. Make a habit of connecting with people actively moving forward. This is a way to make sure you are in the right place at the right time for additional introductions or opportunities to present themselves. By that, I mean you never know who you will get connected to or what opportunities you may stumble across.

Your homework is to start having conversations with people!

Whatever choices you make moving forward, 60s+ Seeker, you seem ready for life's adventures. I believe you will make the best out of whatever you decide.

With love, strength & vigor –

LARA

HOW MUCH WORK

How much do I need to work?

I know, it sounds too simple: enough to pay the bills! But for us worker bees, it's more complicated AND prompts more questions. What constitutes work? What are the numbers, $, bills, discretionary, that would allow me to pull back? Where do obsessive feelings of usefulness take over or take the back seat?

—Janna, 68, Seattle

Dear Janna,

I love how you have shared some complexities that arise for you in your question. There does not need to be any shame in enjoying work. You have identified that you like to feel useful (very human!) I will help you expand your questioning and give you some reframes to carve your own ambitious path forward.

HEAD HEART GUT

Head loves these questions to ruminate on and to latch onto. Head loves feeling useful! Head loves feeling productive and understanding the numbers. Head says that getting these answers figured out is a very smart thing to do.

Heart senses that Head may be getting too much sway here. Heart is tapping you on the shoulder, reminding you that pulling back could also be important. Heart beats a different drum than Head. What will allow you to get to the bottom of this situation? Heart wants to define the problem and the questions clearly so we can get good, useful answers that lead us down our desired path.

Gut is feeling that the question is complicated because it can see Heart wanting more attention. Gut often finds itself going along with Head, getting wrapped up in those feelings from productivity and usefulness. But Gut knows that you have more important questions to ask yourself, otherwise perhaps you would not have written to me.

EXISTENTIAL

Janna, at your beautiful age of 68 years old, I imagine that you have thought more about death and purpose than I have. If you live another ten, twenty, or thirty years, what do you want the story to be? What is the thread of usefulness about in the story of your life?

Existentialism asks us to define our own sense of purpose and to find meaning in our lives. This is no small task and is enough to fill anyone's lifetime.

Here are other questions that come to mind regarding your questions, Janna:

- Do your words and your actions line up?
- What are the pros and cons of pulling back?
- Do you give your time and your focus to the things that you say are important to you?

I ask these things to see how your actions help you feel supported in what you are doing already. What do you need to give yourself permission to do in your life right now?

PROFESSIONAL

Janna, you have brought up several excellent questions and I urge you to answer them. To simplify, I have broken them down into a list:

- What financial situation would allow you to pull back?
- What constitutes work?
- What role does an obsession with usefulness play?

Perhaps a simple answer is enough to quiet the gremlins, to feel useful and fulfilled, but not so much that you overdo it. From a slightly more nuanced perspective, it sounds like you want to pull back from work a bit. If that is the case, then I urge you to put some of your questions aside (tell your Head and thoughts to quiet down a bit!) Don't overthink this.

Action will reveal much more information and feelings than pondering ever will. If you want to work less, do the math, and see what the simplest ways to reduce your workload are. Try it out! How do you feel when you work less? Prototyping, creating mini experiments toward your solutions will reveal your way forward.

From a coach's perspective, prototypes that allow you to experience different workloads are key to getting you to where you want to go. Alongside your prototypes, it would also be helpful to do some coffee chats and informational interviews with other folks in your situation. Make a list of people whose life you admire. Get some coffee dates on the calendar with them and ask some of the following questions:

- How much are you working currently?

- If you have reduced your workload, how did you do that?

- What has been instrumental in your retirement/pulling back/career?

- What has been the most helpful resource in managing your finances?

If it feels appropriate, you can share some of what you're grappling with and ask what they might recommend.

I recommend finding financial management resources and sitting down with someone to help you answer your number questions. The math of this situation may tell you something you don't know or reveal additional options that you weren't clear on yet. Plus, it's an integral part of the picture that you are painting. The answer to your financial questions will help you further flesh out your thoughts and feelings about your other questions.

Your question regarding obsessive feelings about usefulness sound linked to our current capitalist systems, the Western culture of putting work on a pedestal, our modern ideas around we are what we do and other influences such as upbringing, background, etc. If you really want to work more or keep working the same amount but feel guilty about that, then it's time to practice some radical acceptance.

Do you want to grapple with your demons and make some peace with your obsessive feelings about usefulness? There is real work you can do there. These are all great feelings, thoughts, and ideas to pull apart in therapy or with a coach.

To dig deeper, you could do something as simple as a daily audit on when you felt the urge or pressure to be useful versus when it naturally arose or felt good. You could take this further by digging into your upbringing, what your family taught you about work and usefulness, and the ideas you have currently about how members of society should behave and why.

A good homework assignment for analyzing obsessive feelings of usefulness is to research anti-capitalist literature or videos to break down some of our cultural brainwashing. To scrutinize productivity, work, and society, read *Four Thousand Weeks: Time Management for Mortals* by Oliver Burkeman. For more recommendations, look at the Resources List at the back of this book.

Part of my mission is to inspire everyone to be the boss of their own life. *You* are the boss, Janna. What rules do you need to break? And what new rules do you need to write in their place?

With joy & rebellion,

Lara

EFFECTIVITY OVER PRODUCTIVITY

Hey Lara,

My big question about life right now is: How to move from a professional life focused on productivity to one more attuned to effectivity. In other words, not just always doing stuff, but focusing on the important impactful stuff. Sincerely, Canosplat

Dear Canosplat,

I love this question. Not only do I frequently meditate on this question in my life, but I regularly help my clients dissect it. And dissecting an issue is one of my favorite ways of working with people. In some positions there is room to redesign our jobs to be more in alignment with what is important to us. The Big Quit is evidence of people not wanting to stay in jobs that are not in alignment. So, I'll answer your question from the lens of not just always doing stuff in your work to focusing on the important and impactful aspects of your current job.

HEAD HEART GUT

From the sound of it, Head must be tired of banging itself against a wall. I imagine that just doing stuff feels rather frustrating if it is on the regular, especially if it has led you to this question. I love tapping into that brilliant brain of yours and game-ifying how to maximize your productivity. From my experience in online business, productivity is king. Maximize everything! Be productive! This is the best way! Capitalism has brainwashed Head to believe that productivity is the most important measure to focus on. However, Head is often smarter than that.

The Heart says, *Oh yes! Impact baby!* This is good. There's a kind of magic that happens between Head and Heart when we accomplish work that creates impact.

Your Gut is probably saying the same thing: *Let's do this!*

And then there is a pause. YES, we want to focus on the important things that move the needle forward. But how? And what tasks are those exactly?

EXISTENTIAL

What meaning have you assigned to work within the bigger picture of your life? I ask you this because you do not have all the time in the world to figure out the answer. If you want to do more impactful work, take the time to learn about what that means to you. How do you do this?

1. Identify your thoughts, feelings, and values.

2. Define them in a way that makes sense to you (check out the Define My Terms worksheet in the downloadable workbook).

3. Integrate them into your life.

To assign meaning to things, we must carve out the time to genuinely consider open-ended questions. For example, we may uncover some meaning here by going back to the beginning. You mention in your question "productivity" and "just always doing stuff." Journal on the following questions (write for five minutes for each question):

- What is the difference between productivity and just doing stuff?
- What is the difference between productivity and impact?
- What role does productivity have in your life?
- What role does impact have in your life?
- How can you define and prioritize what matters most to you on a more regular basis?
- How will you know when you are doing more impactful work?

If you have the freedom, flexibility, desire, and chutzpah to define and do work that is meaningful to you, then you must do it. To not do it is in bad faith. We need more people doing what lights them up. You will give others permission to assign meaning and purpose to their own work and pave the way for them to focus on what has an impact.

It is actually imperative that you do this. If the thought occurs to you, then you need to take action, otherwise you're doing yourself and others a disservice. Once you connect with the impact of your work, the effectiveness to carry through will come naturally. To enjoy your work for decades to come, pay more attention to what brings you joy and what feels meaningful. Move forward with that awareness and see where it takes you.

PROFESSIONAL

You have got to get crystal clear about what your values are and what constitutes impactful work to you (or to your employer).

Here are the steps to Defining Terms and putting them into action, so that you can focus more on the important tasks at work:

1. Define your terms (see the Define My Terms Worksheet).

2. State your big picture goal.

3. Put systems in place.

4. Get support.

This is your roadmap to learn what impactful work is to you and how to put it into practice. We will start with the Define My Terms Worksheet. I wouldn't say I am a word nerd, but I like words. I like the way they look, and I love figuring out the exact word I want to use to express my desired feelings. I encourage you to lean into whatever aspects of vocabulary that might speak to you here.

For this exercise, you will insert "impactful work" on the Define My Terms worksheet, in the workbook you downloaded. Utilize the prompts on the worksheet to get to the heart of impactful work for you.

Once you have defined your terms and you know what constitutes impactful work, you can begin to see where you should spend your time focusing. In order to better prioritize important tasks and put this information into action, I recommend Googling and completing the Eisenhower Matrix Worksheet.

This Matrix will help you clarify the importance of each task and shed some light on how to eliminate certain things immediately. I would encourage you to share this information with your boss and your team. If you do not have a mentor or someone who is supporting you in growing in your current position, I suggest finding a person to fulfill that role. Sharing this information could be important for the company. This is a clarifying exercise I often use with my clients that can inform your growth within your organization.

You can use steps 2 through 4 of this process regularly to maintain focus on impactful work. Use the Eisenhower Matrix daily. Schedule time for these tools and for accountability on a weekly basis. This will shift your focus from "just doing stuff" to being held accountable toward important and effective tasks.

Use the Define My Terms worksheet in the downloadable Workbook. Also, take a gander at Bold Choice. You have the power to make the changes you seek. Keep going!

With Strength & vigor –

xoxo,
Lara

TIRED DREAMER

I want to change careers (no plan to what yet) but I have a very young family, am sleep deprived/stressed and don't feel I can handle the change now. Let alone invest time in figuring out my next step! I am good at the job I have had for ten years but I want a change eventually. How do I know when to jump off the cliff? I need to be capable of investing time into myself and that time is not now... I'm not the type to handle failure well, so I don't want a false start and I need the energy to break out of the familiar!

XO, Tired Dreamer

Dear Tired Dreamer,

I feel your struggle deeply in my bones. I too have a young family, with toddlers eighteen months apart. Though I switched from being employed with a good job to being self-employed before I had children, I often struggle with the frequent changes and uncertainties of not having stable employment. I understand when you say you do not handle failure well, which I think says a lot about your self-awareness and current needs from your work life.

Now is not the time to make a change. It might simply be the time to plant some seeds. Dreaming of what might be possible in the future may be enough to break you out of the familiar and infuse you with some inspirational energy (even if you don't act on it right now).

Keep in mind there may never really be a good time. Typically, in these situations with a young family and sleep deprivation, there are worse times, but not really good times. As in, there is no good time to have kids, do a 180 in your career, or have a life crisis that upends everything. So, when there are no good times, we have to figure out different choosing criteria. Or, for those of us who are risk averse, choosing to maintain the status quo for as long as possible is also an option. However, there usually comes a time when life is screaming for a change and it may be forced upon you. Don't let it get that bad if you can avoid it. That said, Tired Dreamer, now is definitely not the time. In the future, know that career transitions come in all shapes and sizes.

HEAD HEART GUT

Your Head and Heart are in the right place. Your Gut is saying, *Change has to happen. Eventually.* Your Gut is exhibiting its certainty when you write "that time is not now." Gut sees the sleep deprived fog. It senses the instability of a job change and those signals are telling you to wait. When it is time, Gut will be more awake, more alert, and more curious. Your Gut and your Heart will let you know when it is time. You will feel the flutter of your inquisitive nature and find a resolution to gather energy to make a change.

Your Head may not agree, so be ready for the fight. Head will disagree for a million and one reasons, including things like fear of the unknown, settling for the familiar and being consistently sleep deprived for years! The fight between Head, Heart, and Gut may be a quiet one, where you fantasize about switching jobs, but can't seem to take action. Or perhaps you burn out in your career but use the lack of clarity as an excuse to not take action. Heart will feel flutters of excitement, which will periodically be squashed by Head claiming that your dreams are irrational. Gut will reconnect with inspiration and want to take a leap, but Head might stop you in your tracks. Don't let fear or thoughts of failure win.

To overcome your fears, you must address them. So, when Heart and Gut start yelling at you that it's time to change, listen. You are a brave and curious being that always wants to be learning. Humans have a natural inclination to explore and connect with the world around them. Even though Head wants you to be safe, it also wants to learn and connect. Heart and Gut demand it. To address this directly, put support systems in place. Gather your family, find a coach, hire a headhunter and resume writer, so that you have a whole team of people to help you take the next step in your professional development. You are not the first person to struggle with failure and fear of career transitions - all of us have. This is a good thing! It means that every person on our team can share their stories of transition and guide you through the journey.

EXISTENTIAL

Humans love waiting until we are in dire straits to make big changes. Or waiting for the right time. We hang on to our normal for as long as possible. Once we feel like we can't go on another minute, we might finally relinquish control. It is a difficult thing that we humans must make decisions for ourselves. With no predefined meaning or path in life, creating those things for ourselves becomes overwhelming at times. So, in the case of knowing when to switch jobs or career paths, you must figure this out for yourself to know it is true for you. It could hit you like a ton of bricks one day. Or that moment may never come.

Do not succumb to complacency, to the fast pace of the world, and let the transition pass you by. Making no choice is making a choice. So, make it a conscious one. Hire a coach, talk to a spiritual guide, call your mom, chat with a friend—let people in your life know that you want to make a career change someday and that they can help you stay accountable to it. There is something powerful about stating intentions out loud and asking for support along the way.

PROFESSIONAL

It is our fear of change and our fear of failure (whatever that means in the moment) that holds us back. Your life demands that you become a salmon willing to swim upstream of fear and change to the more desirable waters and breeding grounds of inspired action. Sometimes you have to be scared to even know you're brave. When you recognize your bravery, you will make better decisions for yourself.

On that note, Tired Dreamer, there are no real false starts. Even when it feels like it, know that every action, every experience, is leading you along the beautiful path of your life.

It doesn't have to be a cliff you are jumping off. Sometimes a career change can look like mining your network and realizing there is an opportunity waiting for you there. It could also be finding an open position, applying while you are still comfortable in your current role, and then getting hired somewhere else.

Sometimes, career change comes as a quiet knock at the door, or a gentle job offer from a friend. You never know how these things will unfold. When is the time to make some changes? For now, stay open and allow yourself to brainstorm and fantasize about what may be fun in the future. You could even open up your calendar and schedule a check-in date with yourself one year from now. Perhaps call a friend and ask them about their last career switch and how it came together. You can also use FutureMe.org to write yourself an email to be sent to you at a time in the future. Use this as a tool to remind yourself of your desire for change and to circle back to the question: how will I know when I'm ready?

There are small ways you can start preparing for change now. This will help stave off any desperation or irrational decision-making down the road. Network leveraging is when you take stock of who you know, connect with them deliberately and get to know more people through those you already know. Leveraging your network is just a fancy way of consciously taking the time to catch up with people in your network and doing informational interviews: ask specific questions, learn about new opportunities and events, ask for introductions and resources. Network leveraging can be done at any stage of career and should honestly be a sustained and ongoing practice. What does this mean exactly? It means:

- Talk to people.
- Get their story.
- Take notes.
- Whose life do you admire?
- What jobs sound interesting and fun?
- How did people in interesting & fun fields get to where they are?
- Have conversations and lots of them. Be genuine and curious.
- Make new friends and connections.

This may not lead to a career change now, but you never know who you will meet and in what capacities you may collaborate. Magic happens when people get together and share their stories.

Your homework for now, Tired Dreamer, is to talk to people. Connect with your network, take care of yourself, reflect on what lights you up and how you spend your time. Do the exercises I have listed here. Save this letter and review it in six months to a year. When it is time to make a bigger change, let your questions and curiosity lead the way.

To commitment and rest,

Lara

P.S. I am a certified coach in the SparkeType assessment and encourage you to take their free assessment at Sparketype.com.

ACCEPTED NEW JOB

I accepted a new job that is great for my mental health, but the benefits are not sustainable long term. I was asked to make a two-year commitment. I'm wondering how I can best leverage the opportunity to grow my career while here?

Dear Accepted,

Congratulations! How excellent that you have a job that is great for your mental health. It does sadden me that your particular position isn't supporting you in the ways you need long term. One of my dreams for the future is that all of us will be supported with benefits to live healthy lives no matter what our jobs are. Let's see how we can set you up for success.

HEAD HEART GUT

Head is thrilled that you have landed this position! Of course, it simultaneously is looking out for Number One (you) and is looking down the road: you need better benefits at some point. Head won't let you forget that this probably is not a long-term gig.

Heart is singing your favorite song because even if this does not give you everything you want in life, it is really good right now. Heart may ache a little knowing that it wants a triple win situation, and it had to do some sacrificing for this position.

Gut says, *We did it! We landed the job!* It's helping you feel excited and giving you that rush to do something new. Gut also says, *Let's make it worth it!* This brings with it a weighted sense of responsibility in making the commitment to a new position. It also brings with it an openness to learning. Perhaps Gut is a little nervous about the growth that is desired.

EXISTENTIAL

If we consider the existential philosophy that life is about accepting meaninglessness in order to assign our own authentic meaning, then this moment is about assigning purpose to your current commitment. I feel you have already done this, Accepted, but make sure you have the clarity you want. Take a bird's-eye view of your two-year commitment, assign it a clear purpose that feels authentic to you. Answer these questions:

- Why did you accept this job right now?
- How does this job support your mental health?
- What can you look for in future opportunities to continue supporting your mental health?
- What does success look like in two years?
- What does failure look like?
- What obstacles will get in the way of leveraging your current situation?
- How can you mitigate those obstacles?
- Who will hold you accountable?
- When will you check in on your progress?

You can incorporate the questions into the WOOP Worksheet in the downloadable workbook. These answers will help you be clearer about the purpose these next two years serve and how you can stay committed to your long-term goals. It sounds like you are on an exciting path with lots of interesting opportunities ahead of you.

This time will turn into your life story, and you get to create it. So, what would you like to thank yourself for in the future? Or, what will your future self thank you for working on today?

PROFESSIONAL

You are well on your way, Accepted. Embrace the journey! There may be items specific to your industry to grow your career in the way you would like - and while I may not address those, I can tell you how to find out what they are.

Never underestimate the power of conversation and connection. Your homework while you're in this position for the next two years is to talk to everyone. Build relationships with everyone in your organization and all those that your job connects you to. If you can, go to conferences and industry-related activities. Meet people and maintain a connection with a few of them. Stay in touch with the ones who feel like authentic and strategic connections. Collect and connect with different acquaintances that you can build a networking portfolio with. It is with these people who you should discuss career and industry growth.

Interview your professional network, both at your own company and others, to learn about their career trajectories and how they have made their work work for them. There are also several books and internet resources that discuss growth in your particular industry. Dive into them when you are not nurturing your healthy network of relationships.

Is there anyone at your company who can mentor you? Actively seek that relationship. If there is no such opportunity at this time, see if you can find someone in the same industry who can fulfill that role. Ask the people you trust for feedback. Ask them the best ways to grow in your role. Ask for their stories about how they have been able to grow their careers. You will come across lots of good anecdotal advice from people who are ahead of you.

By building relationships with everyone around you, you are increasing your know, like, and trust factor. This is commonly referred to as the "KLT factor" on the internet and is often associated with branding and networking. The idea is that we work and buy from people, brands, and companies who we know, like, and trust. We are most likely to use a service when we know who that service is run by and or have a positive referral from someone we already know. Similarly, we want to build relationships with brands that we like. Most of us stop going to people or places that we dislike for obvious reasons. However, we may work with a company or a person we don't like, if we know and trust that they will do a good job. So, when you increase your know, like, and trust factor with those in your industry, you are building a strong network of people who are interested in seeing you succeed. Over the next two years, these people are going to become more invested in your life, your work, and how to support you. Now is the time for you to build the bridge to get the benefits you truly desire.

It would be beneficial to build a customer relations management (CRM) database of your own right now, if you are serious about leveraging your network and career. CRMs are typically used for marketing and business owners, but if you can lean into your nerdy side for tracking your relationship-building conversations, that's really all it is. Notion (the app) and others have CRM templates that are easy to use. Google Drive also provides CRM templates. You can enter the people you connect with and have the software notify you when three months have gone by. It will remind you to reach out and reconnect. This way, you are systematically building relationships that will launch you to the next opportunity when the time comes.

Finally, find a way to make your desires over the next two years obvious. Create visual reminders of what you are looking to achieve over the next two years.

I recommend reading *Atomic Habits* by James Clear and applying his principles to your situation. Habit change and behavioral development require that you make your goal or habit easy and obvious.

You can write yourself a letter, fill out a commitment contract (I have one for you in the downloadable workbook), or simply put an affirmation that sums up your goal on a post-it-note. Making your networking efforts measurable can help you track this specific progress.

Scheduling check in's and reflection opportunities will help you stay committed to your goals. These are a few examples of quantifying and tracking your journey.

I'm excited for you, Accepted. I hope that these next couple of years are fun, healthy, and a great opportunity to leverage the work you are doing.

With love, strength, & vigor,

provides CRM templates. You can enter the people you connect with and have the software notify you when three months have gone by. It will remind you to reach out and reconnect. This way, you are systematically building relationships that will launch you to the next opportunity when the time comes.

Finally, find a way to make your desires over the next two years obvious. Create visual reminders of what you are looking to achieve over the next two years.

I recommend reading *Atomic Habits* by James Clear and applying his principles to your situation. Habit change and behavioral development require that you make your goal or habit easy and obvious.

You can write yourself a letter, fill out a commitment contract (I have one for you in the downloadable workbook), or simply put an affirmation that sums up your goal on a post-it-note. Making your networking efforts measurable can help you track this specific progress.

Scheduling check in's and reflection opportunities will help you stay committed to your goals. These are a few examples of quantifying and tracking your journey.

I'm excited for you, Accepted. I hope that these next couple of years are fun, healthy, and a great opportunity to leverage the work you are doing.

With love, strength, & vigor,

IT'S A JOB

Hi Lara!

So: my job is kind of awesome. It's creative, challenging, kind of fighting climate change, and it pays pretty well. I'd say it has to be in the top 0.01% of all possible jobs for me and I feel lucky to have it. On the other hand, it's a job. Not my thing. It eats up a ton of my energy, time, and ultimately, I get a paycheck. How do I balance my desire for more? More: meaning, ownership, wealth vs. counting blessings?

Love, Sam

Dear Sam,

I meet so many people who struggle throughout their careers that your question is a good reminder of the wide variety and complexities of work and life. It is also a good reminder that even when things are good, there can still be an additional caveat or underlying sticking point. No one thing fills us up 100%. Even with the most brilliant, well-matched jobs, partners or situations, humans will inevitably come across obstacles.

HEAD HEART GUT

Head is probably running all the math, calculating the percentage of how lucky you are and the aspects of getting more meaning, ownership, and wealth.

Heart knows that jobs aren't really your thing and feels a yearning for the more that is possible.

Gut understands that it has it real good. It gobbles up the blessings while feeling the pangs of the hunger for more. Gut hears Heart's desire and is mulling over how it can go from good to great.

EXISTENTIAL

I love that you feel lucky. This tells me you've created something beautiful. You have worked hard to get to where you are, find value in what you do, and you count your blessings. That's important because so many of us do not and it sucks when we don't. Celebrating what you have been able to create in your life and where things are good is essential. It's challenging to sit with and celebrate wins, so I want to make space for it here.

I also want to see you in your desire for more. You know in your heart of hearts that you feel stuck in the current confines of your job. You recognize that there is a balance that you need to strike, and you are reaching out to find it.

My dad has always said that if you can find work that you enjoy 60% of the time and hate 40% of the time, then that is a great balance. Or is it the other way around? Anyway, his perspective is that nothing is perfect, there will always be downsides to every situation, and that tipping the scales even slightly more in your favor is basically winning the life lottery. I have thought about this a lot since he shared it with me. I definitely struggle accepting it knowing I have drunk the "love what you do" Kool-Aid. However, I feel that there is wisdom in it and find that so much of our work as humans is to accept. Which leads me to wondering: how can we accept and strive for more at the same time? You mention striking a balance. I imagine that having this pretty awesome job is the parameter that will force you to be extremely creative in finding ways to make it even better. Humans have a lot of loss aversion, so how can we hold on to what you have while making space for something greater?

PROFESSIONAL

Sam, you have a few things going on: having a job and yearning for more, while also struggling with having a job at all, because "it's not your thing." Since you have created a life and career that you genuinely enjoy much of, you will have to stretch your self-awareness and understanding to level up. To do this, you must define your terms in a way that is authentic. Your definitions must resonate with you deeply so that they inspire you to keep stretching toward what you truly desire. The terms from your question that you must define are *meaning, ownership, and wealth.* Complete the Define My Terms worksheet to get started.

Once you have figured out what these words really mean to you, both philosophically, but also in the physical world, we can expand on each of them. I would encourage you to do a brainstorming exercise. You could mind map or make a simple list.

An assignment I give many of my clients is the 100 Ideas list. I've included this in the downloadable PDF that comes with this book. Write out 100 Ideas, actions, experiments, conversations, connections, etc. ways that you could move your life in the direction of meaning and ownership.

We often get stuck on one solution to our problem when we are thinking about how to transform our situation. Brainstorming exercises are useful in showing us that there are many ways we could create movement toward a solution. And it is likely that the outcome of these actions would lead us to many solutions, depending on which one works out.

In the *Designing Your Life* book, the authors call this phenomenon of getting stuck on one solution "anchor problems." This keeps us stuck thinking that it is the only way forward when there are many other options around us. When it comes to anchor problems, let go of the solution you keep grasping at, but that isn't really possible.

From your question, it sounds like you do not want to have a job, but you need one to live. If your solution is simply not having a job, that may be an anchor problem, especially if you have no other sources of income and want to live an independent life. *Is the solution you are going after currently viable?* If it's impossible, what else are you left with? How can you pursue the meaning, ownership, and wealth that you desire? You need to let go of impossible solutions so that you can re-define your problem and find solutions that are immediately actionable.

An example of an anchor problem could be having a job, the solution you are stuck on is not having a job when you currently still need one to survive. However, reframing the problem of gaining meaning, ownership, and wealth turns things around quite a bit. There are many more solutions here than I have a job, but I don't want one.

Once you have filled out your 100 Ideas Worksheet, pick one to three ideas and see how you can experiment with them in your current situation. Worksheets like Bold Choice, Pros and Cons, and Prototyping will guide you to finding actionable ways of moving forward. Reflect and repeat!

Keep striving for answers, Sam.

With love, strength, & vigor,

LARA

Mauerpark Mural in the Castro of San Francisco 2020

FEAR OF NO INCOME

Hey Lara,

I want to leave my job to start my own business. How do I handle the fear of no income?

Hi Fear of No Income,

This fear makes perfect sense and is totally normal. It is wise to fear no income, as you probably have many bills to pay and potentially, other people to support. Perhaps by acknowledging that the fear you have is healthy and coming from a place with real consequences, you can plan and strategize what your life requires at the moment and how you might be able to start a business.

HEAD HEART GUT

Head says, *I want, I want, I want,* and *I need, I need, I need.* Head also says, *Are you crazy?! We need income!*

Heart says, *Wouldn't it be lovely if we lived in a world where you weren't measured or valued by your ability to produce things? To make money? Wouldn't it be amazing to take regular creative sabbaticals to rest and to do whatever your heart desired?* Yes, that would be lovely. How nice it would be to live in that world.

Gut says, *Oof.* Gut always feels the weight and the brunt of these things. It knows the inescapable truths of life. Gut can sense the future of a life with no income. It feels the hunger. Gut feels unstable when stability is threatened or taken away. Gut measures the uncertainty of an idea. It also feels the excitement, the drama, and the thrilling adventure of embarking on such a journey.

If you really, really, really want to start your own business, check in with your Gut. It's probably been barking at you with a bullhorn already. Gut tells you how badly you want it. Do you want it so badly that it makes your stomach hurt?

When we avoid doing the work we feel compelled to do, we feel it in our bodies. The work that we *can't not do* is the work that you *have to do.* But not just have to, it is the work that is your calling. You can't get away from this kind of work. It can be a passion project that you always make time for, it can be a hobby you are devoted to, or a volunteer labor of love. The point is, you can't *not do it.* You have to do it. And so, your body finds ways of sending you that message.

If you want to build your own business, then Gut will let you know that you have to get cracking. This may come as deep desire, a nauseated yearning, or itchy excitement. It might be something that terrifies you, but you know you have to do it anyway.

I always think about self-supported bicycle trips I have taken. For example, I cycled from Cedar City, Utah to Taos, New Mexico in 2011. I spent the first week biking with my dad. He headed back home when we made it to Durango, Colorado, and I cycled on alone from there. I had so many nerves, those days leading up to the trip and then especially getting on the saddle after saying goodbye to my dad. But I wouldn't abandon my mission! It was a heart-led expedition that needed to be completed, even when I thought I would be eaten by mountain lions in the high desert or struck by lightning during a storm. Your body, your Gut will let you know when a project is exciting enough to pursue even in the face of doubt.

How does this yearning show up for you? What signals are you receiving?

You don't need to give up your income to start your own business. I'd love to hear what your Gut says when you work on your side hustle or your business with a healthy income stream.

EXISTENTIAL

Consider these questions to move forward in life with less regrets:

- What is the work you can't not do? As in: what is the work that you *have to do in this lifetime?*
- What will you regret if you don't try it?
- What do you already regret?

Reflect on your regrets and think about what the deeply important lessons are in these stories. Use the Transforming Regret Worksheet to guide you through this exercise. Your life is trying to teach you something. Your life wants to give you gold, but you have to do the work to find it.

Another exercise to do for additional clarity is the 100 Ideas brainstorming game. Make a 100 ideas list for how to move you from where you are to where you want to go. What is the smallest step you can take? What's the craziest thing you could do? Here are some ideas to get you started:

- Take a vacation.
- Notify your boss that you're quitting.

- Interview for new jobs.
- Take a foundations of business class.
- Interview people who have started the type of business you want to start.
- Open an Etsy store.

What would *future you* thank *present you* for? Run with that. Go make it happen, I believe in you.

PROFESSIONAL

You live in a capitalist society that demands you have an income. Capitalism measures your worth by income. You need money coming from somewhere to meet your deepest needs. You can't do valuable work in the world if you don't get your own basic needs met. So, keep that income, wherever it comes from, that's important.

Starting your own business can look great professionally. It can also be a complete disaster. What are you looking to accomplish on your career path? Do you want an epic rollercoaster journey? Serial job hopping, starting side hustles, launching a business and the like are all excellent ways to have a thrilling career portfolio.

Starting a business is a long and arduous process. Our instant-gratification culture, spreading like wildfire across the internet, would have you believe you can make seven figures with the snap of your pretty manicured nails. But you know how you get pretty manicured fingers? With a paycheck.

This is not meant to discourage you. It's meant to give you clarity. Your question is how to handle the fear of no income. Dig into your finances to understand what you need to get by.

Also, answer these questions:

- What can you live without?
- How much income do you need?
- Who else is a part of this picture?
- What level of say do they get?

You handle the fear of no income by answering the questions that come up around money in your day-to-day life. Then, you either do it because you can or because it's your calling - it's simply the work that you *have* to do in the world. Or you don't because you've realized through doing the math that you have other priorities.

I want to hold your hand right now. I know what it's like to dream of starting your own business. I know what it's like to think about it all the time. I know what it's like to feel stuck and meaningless in certain positions. It's frustrating, draining, exhausting, soul-sucking, and just so freaking hard. But you know what? There's always a way out. "This too shall pass" - best said with Lord of the Rings' boldness and ambiance. *You are not alone.*

The fear of no income is universal. The fear of no income is always present with those of us who give even a scrap of fucks about money. Did you know that people with millions of dollars still worry about money security?

Humans have been blessed with amazing imaginations. Lively. Out of this world, expansive! We've also been gifted with a negativity bias. Now put those two gems together.

Everyone has fears about no income! You can have income one day and have your life turned upside down the next! Remember March of 2020?! Good Lord, what the hell?!

You want to start a business. So here are some more reflection questions to answer:

- What fears do you have around money?
- How can you start a business *and* keep your paycheck?
- What is your easiest or simplest actionable item that could generate income?
- What can you do today to learn more about what it would take to start your business?
- Who can you talk to who was once walking your very same path?

I believe you can start a business if that is what you truly want to do. You can start a business and keep the job that gives you an income. Or you quit your current position and do your business full time. I'm a firm believer in where there's a will, there's a way. There is simply a whole lot of figuring-it-out in between.

A PERSONAL STORY:

I coach my younger sister sometimes. We've coached together for years now. We have lived together, book clubbed together, and yes, I have coached her on personal and professional ventures. My younger sister, Salome, is a badass. She gets shit done. Salome quit her job in New York City and moved in with me in San Francisco. She wrote out a business plan and opened her own café in San Francisco (formerly known as Mauerpark in the Castro). Not only was it a bureaucratic nightmare, but as a solopreneur, there are so many hats you have to wear. So many things that you are responsible for. And there's no one coming to save you. You are the first and the last stop.

When I coached with Salome, many times we would land on this: would you regret it if you didn't go for it? Regret is an excellent teacher; dare I say the best. And if you read Dan Pink's, *The Power of Regret* you know that typically people regret things that they *didn't pursue* more often than the things that they did. Doing things gives us deep experiential knowledge. And once we know, we know. We can often walk away in the aftermath with more clarity and confidence because at least we tried.

There are so many frustrating stories and difficult times in the brief history of Mauerpark, Salome's café. It closed in early 2021 because of the pandemic. Unfortunately, it wasn't an endeavor that came to a peaceful conclusion. It came with a lot of tumult, heartbreak, and foggy San Francisco days, tugging on all our heartstrings. I painted a mural on one of the coolest, busiest little street corners of Mauerpark. Right on a bike path. The next business that took over the space painted over it. There was no loving goodbye with a bow. It was messy and depressing.

The point is, Fear of No Income, is that even though business stories are often messy, Salome still says that what needed to happen *happened*. It wasn't easy. There are a lot of regrets, but at least she tried. To this day, Salome says she would have regretted not opening the café. She also wouldn't do it the same a second time around. Learning through the project gave her the most powerful clarity, and she learned through trying.

Courageously,

POSITIVE IMPACT

How do I find work that has a positive impact on the world while also giving myself time for self-care and flexibility?

Dear Positive Impact,

Ah, yes! A million-dollar question for adults everywhere! I am immediately reminded of a meme that summarizes how I feel about modern existence. It reads: "just to confirm... Everyone feels tired ALL the time no matter how much sleep they get or caffeine they consume, but also has trouble falling asleep/is constantly hungry but also nauseous with acid reflux/spends every second working or cleaning yet nothing gets accomplished?"

While our struggles are nothing new in the face of history, there is a modern overwhelm that is absolutely real. So, while humans have been seeking meaningful work for centuries and looking to improve our quality of daily life, the influx of and access to information has overwhelmed our senses to the point of never feeling relaxed. Our three lenses will help us dissect the issue further and give you specific actions to take.

HEAD HEART GUT

Sometimes Head convinces us that having one thing automatically excludes another. With your question, Head may believe that finding work that has a positive impact on the world means giving up the time you have for self-care and flexibility. Head is right in that it does take time and energy to find work. Self-care requires the same. Your question is an opportunity for Head to uncover its needs and desires around work, as well as how it defines self-care. This is a good time to practice creativity and consider where work and self-care may even overlap.

Heart says, *Doing work I believe is positive is self-care as long as I have boundaries.* Heart also says, *I will show you the way.* Your question is coming from your Heart and it deserves a well thought out answer. It is likely that you need time and space to allow Heart's answers to come to you. Heart says, *Start with what you know.*

As someone who has built their career on helping others figure out the question of doing good work, I believe that self-care is extremely important. It is often when we have time to relax, dream, and have fun that we discover clarity and purpose. I would also argue that self-care has a positive impact on the world. You need to take care of yourself first and foremost. It's just like the oxygen mask on the plane: put yours on before helping others.

As the mom of my two toddlers, I am noticing how much grouchier I am when my self-care goes out the window. I know in my heart of hearts that being an attentive, engaged, and loving parent to my children has a positive impact on the world. I also know that if I do not engage in rejuvenating activities for myself that my mental health plummets. With my husband in a medical residency program, time is in short supply in our household. There are cycles where we simply do what we need to to get by. Other times, we have more flexibility to catch up on sleep or participate in a pickleball game. When we have more gas in our tank, we have more flexibility to spread our positive energy around. This may be in your work and or in your home.

Gut says, *I'm ready for anything once we connect to what positive and impactful work means*. Gut is going to let you know loud and clear when you aren't taking enough time to take care of yourself. Gut will also begin to squeeze you when it isn't getting the amount of flexibility that it likes to have. That's the short of it.

Michael Gershon along with many scientists call the Gut our second brain. Now that is a pretty big statement to make. When your body sends you signals, they are worth paying attention to. Gut is basically where your spidey senses reside and how your body signals to you, *Hey! Something is up! Pay attention*. There are also studies linking our gut health to mental health. Considering the wealth of scientific information coming out about your Gut, let us respect its messages.

First, we need to get all our systems (Head, Heart and Gut) onboard around what positive impact means in our work. Second, we need to assess our personal knowledge of our energy levels and boundaries. How aware are you of your boundaries? Do you know how much self-care and flexibility you need already or is that a question mark at the moment? Gut knows these things, but has it connected with Head and Heart?

Heart and Gut want to convey all this information to Head in a way that is understandable and actionable. Because of that, we will use the remaining sections to further introduce techniques to uncover your beliefs, self-knowledge, and ways to connect your Head to the rest of your body.

EXISTENTIAL

You have got to understand your reasons for living and working to get a better understanding of the questions you truly want to know the answers to. I recommend reading *Designing Your Life* by Bill Burnett and Dave Evans and specifically doing the work-view and life-view exercises. These questions bring the existential into much sharper focus, providing thought-provoking questions like "what is work for? How does it relate to the individual, others, society? What do experience, growth and fulfillment have to do with it?" The goal in doing this is to gain a deeper and more purposeful understanding of the life you want to build and why.

The existential perspective centers on the idea of individual responsibility, authenticity, and the search for meaning in one's life. It asks you to assign your own personal meaning and values to situations and experiences in an otherwise unpredictable world. Based on this viewpoint, finding impactful work involves acknowledging that you have freedom of choice, the power to shape your career path, and to contribute meaningfully to the world. To do this, it is essential to explore your personal values and to understand which careers not only align with you but express your authentic self.

In the search for meaning, we need to weigh our personal values against societal expectations and our financial needs. Existentialism suggests that when we uncover our true values, we implement them and live in alignment with them. This presents some unique challenges when we feel our values around work and self-care are not aligned.

Existentialism says that it is our personal responsibility to take care of our own well-being. Which also means finding meaning in our acts of self-care. In this way, Positive Impact, you are the center of your own existence, and your existence calls for your active engagement in nurturing your own self-care.

Modern society allows us the time and space to consider what a more purposeful career is and how to get it. Humans continue to dream of a better world and to participate in establishing change. However, even though new technologies and tools, like the internet, are helpful in creating change faster,

Gut says, *I'm ready for anything once we connect to what positive and impactful work means.* Gut is going to let you know loud and clear when you aren't taking enough time to take care of yourself. Gut will also begin to squeeze you when it isn't getting the amount of flexibility that it likes to have. That's the short of it.

Michael Gershon along with many scientists call the Gut our second brain. Now that is a pretty big statement to make. When your body sends you signals, they are worth paying attention to. Gut is basically where your spidey senses reside and how your body signals to you, *Hey! Something is up! Pay attention.* There are also studies linking our gut health to mental health. Considering the wealth of scientific information coming out about your Gut, let us respect its messages.

First, we need to get all our systems (Head, Heart and Gut) onboard around what positive impact means in our work. Second, we need to assess our personal knowledge of our energy levels and boundaries. How aware are you of your boundaries? Do you know how much self-care and flexibility you need already or is that a question mark at the moment? Gut knows these things, but has it connected with Head and Heart?

Heart and Gut want to convey all this information to Head in a way that is understandable and actionable. Because of that, we will use the remaining sections to further introduce techniques to uncover your beliefs, self-knowledge, and ways to connect your Head to the rest of your body.

EXISTENTIAL

You have got to understand your reasons for living and working to get a better understanding of the questions you truly want to know the answers to. I recommend reading *Designing Your Life* by Bill Burnett and Dave Evans and specifically doing we still need to put in the work (like finding and getting new jobs). In line with existential philosophies around creating and defining meaning on an individual level, the internet can give you all the information you could ever want and more, but it is still up to you to decipher and discern how it all fits into your life.

Similarly, the internet can provide you with hours of entertainment and tools for self-care (think meditation apps and relaxing bath recipes), but it can also eat up all of your self-care time if you're not careful. This is only one example of how individuals need to work on setting their own personal boundaries and then hold them. This is no easy feat. When it comes to impactful work, which may mean working for a nonprofit organization or other company that asks a lot of you, it can be hard to say no. Startups notoriously also blur the lines between work, leisure, and having a life.

When it comes to building a legacy, existentialism says that defining your reasons for living and how you would like to express those things is essential. Rather than conform to external standards of positive impact, you must define what that means for your life and live in accordance with your authentic self. Additionally, you must consider the inherent ambiguity and uncertain nature of life. Though you may strive to have a positive impact on the world, life often lacks clear-cut answers or directions. Incorporate the winding nature of your life's journey while embracing personal responsibility, the creation of meaning, and ethical considerations.

PROFESSIONAL

Start by writing a single sentence that encompasses your definition of positive impact. Next, write a list of three people you know who are doing work that you believe to have a positive impact on the world. If you don't know three people in this category of your life, find three examples of people who you do not yet know but believe to be doing work similar to what you might like to be doing. Create a template email telling your three impactful workers why you admire what they do and inquire if you could interview them about their job for 20 minutes. Make sure to personalize these emails and send them out. When you interview the people whose work you admire, make sure to ask them how they incorporate self-care and flexibility into their lives.

In addition to these informational interviews, do research on careers you believe to be impactful. Reach out to people who have those jobs or work for those companies. Glassdoor and LinkedIn are excellent resources to learn more about organizations and make direct contact with employees. 80,000 Hours is another great resource that addresses impact and goodness in occupations specifically. They even offer one free coaching session through their website. I myself have reached out to friends of friends and cold-messaged new connections to learn more about a specific career or company. People love to share their stories and knowledge when and where they can.

Many cities have forward-thinking organizations that help you make connections to community resources. The Alliance Center in Denver, Colorado, provides speed-networking events for everyday citizens to get to know one another and expand their network. There are always several people who are looking for new career opportunities there. The Alliance Center also works with environmental and social justice organizations.

Sustainable Connections in Bellingham, Washington, provides a directory of environmentally friendly businesses around town. They also host events showcasing businesses and a wide range of community projects. I encourage you to find a place like this near to you and see how they can support you.

In all aspects of life, it is very important to get clear about what words mean to you. Define what you mean when you say "positive impact" and then see if you can speak with even more clarity. Spend time answering the following questions. Your question really comes down to clarity of terms. Reflect on what comes out and how you can refine what you are asking for.

- What does positive impact mean to you?
- What is work that has a positive impact on the world?

Positive impact is nuanced because some solutions create other problems or don't address all sides of one problem. It also doesn't put a dent in what your strengths and propensities are. Are you a people person or do you prefer to work mostly solo? Many people get sucked into doing work that they are good at or that comes easily to them but hate their day-to-day tasks. Are you willing to work any job simply because it falls into your category of having a positive impact on the world?

Ideally, start working on a Venn diagram of what you are good at, what you want to do, and what is needed in the world. The overlap of the three circles holds the answer to your question, or at the very least gives you a good direction to start heading in.

Consider the following questions to start building your Venn diagrams:

- What are my greatest strengths?
- What am I good at?
- What am I curious about?
- What do I love doing even if I'm not good at it?

- What is the best job I've ever had? What was so great about it?

- What was the worst job? Write down the pros and cons about it too.

- What do you believe is deeply needed in the world?

- What are your greatest concerns for humanity?

Keep in mind that being a better version of yourself, being a happier and healthier human, is making a positive impact on the world. The more taken care of you are, the more you can take care of others.

You can do a deep dive into defining good impactful work and use the resources from 80,000 Hours, an amazing nonprofit organization that encourages people to pursue work that is good for the rest of the planet. They have aggregated as much scientific research as possible about the impact of different industries.

From a simplistic standpoint, start time chunking. Allocate specific chunks of time to specific tasks. It is a productivity tool that follows the philosophy that if you schedule time for something, then you are more likely to do it. Time chunk and follow your schedule. Perhaps you have a full-time job, and you can only realistically search for other jobs for one or two hours a couple of days a week. Schedule those hours into your weekly calendar and make sure to put in the time.

Here are your homework assignments:

- Schedule research sessions 2-3 times a week (20 mins to one hour) to talk to people and get your documents in order. And I don't mean to do all of those things in that one hour. I mean, take that one hour and work on what you can. Maybe it is simply having one conversation.

- Take one hour a couple of times a week, maybe Mondays and Wednesdays to do self-care and be flexible.

- Find an accountability partner who you can check in with about these assignments and review how it is going (or hire a coach, like me!)

I think you will find that if you follow your scheduled (or unscheduled) activities and are present with yourself when you are practicing self-care, you can create a life that has time for work, self-care, and flexibility. No matter what you choose, remember: whatever you are, be a good one.

With conviction & commitment,

xoxo ,

LARA

P.S. If you haven't done so already, read the Effectivity Over Productivity letter.

P.P.S. Download the Workbook and use the worksheets to help answer all of these questions, plus check out the Resources section in the back of this book for more information.

LIFE, DEATH, AND WEIRD

"We're all water from different rivers, that's why it's so easy to meet; we're all water in this vast, vast ocean, someday we'll evaporate together."

– Yoko Ono

SELF-CARE

What should a self-care routine look like?

-Erica

Dear Erica,

What a lovely and practical question. When I read it, I remembered that self-care *can* be routine! And then I think, *Now isn't that a great idea!*

HEAD HEART GUT

Head will have you thinking that self-care is a bubble bath with a scented candle, preferably a scene you can post on Instagram. However, self-care for Head may actually be some guided meditation, a conversation with a therapist or good friend, and getting away from all the screens in your life.

Heart needs time in nature, a mindfulness practice, and something that makes you feel connected to something bigger than yourself. Heart longs for connection and awe. A self-care routine is led by Heart. That means that whatever the routine ends up being, your Heart feels lighter afterward, and the proceeding calm radiates to Head and Gut. Ask Heart what it wants in a self-care routine. Start there.

Gut loves a massage, exercise, and dancing (or whatever might feel wild and free to you). Gut loves a good soak in a warm bath, is down to hit the spa, or gets in a sweat session at a local fitness studio. Gut wants to feel connected to Heart and seen by Head. Gut wants you to know that your body is the vessel that carries your Head, Heart, and all the rest - so please listen to what it has to say and how it feels.

A self-care routine can look like honoring these parts of yourself in different ways throughout the week. Or it can look like a daily practice that combines all three. Start with Heart. Let it be the designer. Give yourself some space to brainstorm what feels exciting to you. This may also look like acknowledging what already exists in your life that feels rejuvenating to you.

EXISTENTIAL

Take care of yourself or do not. Let us take a page from the Star Wars saga when Yoda says, "Do or do not. There is no try." If you are committed to taking care of yourself, do the small and big things to take care of yourself. You must do this because no one else can truly do it for you, and at the end of the day, you are all that you have. If you do not take care of yourself, you won't be around to take care of others.

When you take an action, commit to it fully. Committing to your self-care may be in small actions or big ones, but your life depends on *the doing*. Even small things can make incremental differences in life. In the words of Ocean Vuong: *when the apocalypse comes, what will you put into the vessel of the future?*

PROFESSIONAL

As your coach, I'd reflect this question right back at you. What do you love doing for yourself? What are your guilty pleasures?

What are the activities that relax you? What do you want more of but never make the time for? Do you like baths? Do you get enough sleep? What's your stance on massage? What's your budget?

I would encourage you to have an arsenal of self-care routines.

Create a 2-minute action that checks the self-care box daily when you don't have time for more. Here's a quick exercise to help you create a self-care box that can be checked off within two minutes:

- Brainstorm somewhere between 10 and 100 ideas of what you like to do for self-care.
- Pick three you can do in a 2-minute window.
- Figure out a 2-minute action for each self-care exercise.
- Choose one of the three and practice it for 30 days.
- Reflect on how that makes you feel.
- Reflect, edit, experiment, repeat.

Here are some examples of a 2-minute self-care routine:

- While you make your morning tea or coffee, stretch for two minutes in whatever way feels good to you.
- Meditate for two minutes before getting out of the car to go to work.
- When you find yourself at a desk with a pen, doodle for a while.
- Keep a gratitude journal before you tuck yourself in at night.

I suggest having a list of self-care routines to choose from that can fill different chunks of time and rejuvenate different parts of yourself. Have a small but substantial routine that is regenerative and fuels your spirit. Have a grand self-care gesture that feels super luxurious, but perhaps you only get to once a month or even once a year. Spoil yourself rotten.

From a professional standpoint, we can break this into many comprehensive facets. There are self-care routines you may not like that much but are so important. This could be everything from washing your face, brushing your teeth, working out, sleeping enough, and eating healthy. There are self-care routines that check some of these boxes, but we don't always have a regular time for such as a dance or aerialist class, making art, doing puzzles, and community bike rides. There's the luxurious solo time that may include massage, tarot readings, and long essential oil-filled baths.

Whatever the activities are, find the ones that are regenerative to you. They have got to fill you up. They have got to connect you back to you. For me personally, I need self-reflection time and time with good friends. Journaling helps keep me sane and grounded. Having lunch or dinner with friends gives me time to decompress, laugh, and be in the community.

These routines can change. You would be wise to be flexible and honor your psyche's feedback on this one. Sometimes you desperately need company, and sometimes you need to be alone. Learn as much as you can about yourself in these routines. Then supercharge yourself on purpose: schedule the time for these activities and honor the schedule. This means to do the thing you said you were going to do at the time you said you would. That is how you take care of yourself regularly. That is how you supercharge yourself.

Additionally, utilize habit stacking to incorporate self-care into your daily routine. Habit stacking is when you couple your new desired behavior with something already a habit and routine in your life. For example, when you are sipping your morning coffee, take an extra minute to do a mindfulness practice. When you arrive home from work, do a breath or writing exercise to center yourself before getting out of the car. Find actions that you already do that give you an opportunity to do self-care.

A self-care routine should look like something doable, and make you feel more like yourself. Ideally, it is a regenerative activity, especially over time. Regenerative like eating a healthy lunch, exercising, meditation, reflection, stretching, and spending time outdoors. Self-care can take any form if it makes you feel cared for. Make it routine by making it achievable in your daily life and by coupling it with an action already in your schedule (think shower, coffee, entering and exiting spaces, etc.). Develop your routine from there.

You're worth it, Erica.

With love & care,

GIVE UP

How do you know when to give up a dream to make way for something else?

-Hope

Dear Hope,

This is such a beautiful and melancholy question. It often weighs heavily on my mind. I think back to my decision to switch from art to coaching in 2017 and then moving from San Francisco to Denver. It was and still is a time where I feel I closed a lot of doors to open new ones.

My husband, Adrian and I were literally in the middle of ordering coffee at a café in Oakland when he got a phone call from the University of Colorado, inviting him to come study medicine at Anschutz. This was a big deal because Adrian was on two waitlists for admission, and we had been waiting for months to see if anything would materialize. We were actually planning a move to Cleveland for him to pursue an accelerated masters in BioStatistics when we received this call. Adrian readily accepted the offer, to which they replied, "Great! Can you be here in two days?"

I cried a lot that day. Yes, some tears of joy and excitement, but a lot of tears grieving our lives in the Bay Area knowing how long the road is to become a doctor.

I think of this experience because to me it encompasses the duality expressed in your question. When you choose one thing or experience, you say no to others. Humans are hard-wired for loss aversion: the pain of losing something is twice as powerful as gaining the same thing. It's hard to *let go* of whatever you already have and have put a lot of work into.

Losing my life in San Francisco was extremely painful, especially not knowing what the future held for me in Denver. It required a big leap of faith to pursue my committed relationship with Adrian in a new city. If your hand is not being forced, perhaps you can wait and see what additional information is coming your way to help you make this decision over time.

HEAD HEART GUT

Head is probably screaming at you that you're a failure and that you should have given up ages ago. No? Just me? Head is running the pro/con lists and looking for more reasons to decide one way or another. Head is probably exhausted from weighing the options and from spending so much energy on the topic, but it is passionate about finding the best outcome. Head also has a few alarm bells going off, Head says, *Oh no! We can't Lose! Hold on tighter! We put so much work into that!*

Heart says, *Time will tell.* Or does Heart secretly already have a strong opinion that Head cannot accept yet? Heart is always whispering and dropping cute little hints for you to find. These messages can be found in serendipitous conversations, an idea that comes to you in the shower, or in a dream. Heart doesn't want to let go of everything it has worked hard for, but Heart knows that there is always room for more (more projects, more love, more work, more passion.)

Gut feels queasy because the whole body registers that loss aversion! Losing things feels physically painful, in your Gut, in your Heart, and in your mind. Gut may very well still be on the fence about how to proceed. Gut is feeling Head's fatigue. If Heart knows which way to go, Gut says, *Let's make this decision and get it over with.* If clarity is lacking, Gut says, *Let's wait a while. When we know the way, we will let go or recommit.*

EXISTENTIAL

A few other clarifying lenses could come from regret and death. Not knowing the particulars, I'll paint some broad strokes with these reflection questions:

- Will you regret leaving this dream behind?

- Zoom out! What does this dream look like two years from now? What does regret have to teach you in this scenario? What does pride, joy, and well-being teach you?

- If you died within the next five years, how would death change your perspective?

- How do you think about this dream when you consider your lifespan?

Even though humans have a lot of loss aversion, we are amazingly resilient. We anticipate being miserable when we lose something. This is exacerbated by not considering what we have to gain from a situation that we see as bad. Research shows that after difficult events, when we have had time to process our feelings, we often find ways to rationalize and explain why what we have ended up with is actually the best outcome. It's kind of a secret superpower.

PROFESSIONAL

I had an experience with my coach, Bear Hebert, spending our hour together discussing exactly this topic. How do you know? When is it time? The answer is: you don't. Or rather - you will. Which means - You *will know* when *you know. There will come a time when clarity strikes.* Or perhaps that time will never come, but other things will become clearer which may force the decision if there is still one to be made. There are plenty of well-organized resources for decision-making, like *The Decision Book* and the Bento Box tool. However, for the sake of time, here are a few things to consider a start/stop/continue scenario with your question:

- How urgent is getting an answer to this question?

- If you need to make a decision soon (financial, a deadline, systems pressure, external sources, other people, etc.), then write out a pro and con list or use the Bento Box technique.

- A more involved tool, if it seems relevant, are the Odyssey Plans from the *Designing Your Life* book. You can find free templates online.

- I also suggest writing a letter to this project and seeing what comes up for you. Is it a breakup letter filled with agony? Or is it a letter brimming with grit and commitment? Write the letter from the standpoint of a friend speaking to another person.

Know that whatever ends up transpiring, Hope, you will find a way to make the best of it.

With love, strength, & vigor,

XOXO, *Lara* ♥

LET GO

How can I learn to 'let go?' Of: stuff, habits, obsessions, regrets, and anything else that no longer serves me? To make room for new ideas and create space for what I am keeping.

-Rachel

Dear Rachel,

Letting go is a lifelong process. It's like cleaning or organizing. Letting go is a meditation, an act that we have to keep practicing, always. I say this and at the same time am thinking, *aaaaaahhhhhhh! I don't know!!!* Personally, I find that time is the most reliable partner for letting go.

HEAD HEART GUT

Head: *Hahaha, make me.*
Heart: *There's always space here.*
Gut: *Make space and leave room for pie.*

EXISTENTIAL

Have fun with it! If you like reading, *The Life Changing Magic of Tidying Up* by Marie Kondo is all about *joy.* Can you make *joy* the centerpiece of this exercise? Can you make wholehearted living the theme? Perhaps when you let go of letting go, you'll find that what you need is right in front of you.

PROFESSIONAL

There are real exercises you can do to learn how to let go. Meditation and guided audios come to mind, my personal favorite being the Headspace app. There are also professional organizers, books, websites, and techniques for organizing and reducing what you own.

Are you familiar with Marie Kondo's *The Art of Tidying Up*? She will tell you exactly what you need to do and how to increase joy in your life at the same time!

As far as habits, obsessions, and regrets, I suggest the blog *Zen Habits* by Leo Babauta and *Tiny Habits* by CJ Boggs. Obsessions and regrets make great fodder for enlightening therapy. Consider doing a few sessions to see what it can uncover for you. Many times, having an honest and vulnerable conversation is enough to move your energy and make some space for something new. Which reminds me of Brene Brown's *Atlas of the Heart,* where she explores the complexities of our human nature and focuses on expanding emotional vocabulary.

Let go or be dragged,

P.S. Read the *Give Up* letter on page 183.

SCREEN TIME

What can I do to use what I am good at (analysis) and not spend so much time on the bloody computer?!

-Maggie

Dear Maggie,

Oooh, this is a messy one. I say that because modern life has gotten so nuanced and tech-heavy. It is very challenging these days to limit our computer and screen time. We often end up trading one screen for another and then find ourselves drained. And being drained is not good for decision-making.

HEAD HEART GUT

Head knows that it is good at analytical work and feels drained from too much time on the computer. Head loves being good at things! Head prefers to stay in the safe lane of sticking with what it is good at, rather than putting itself in the scary position of making changes. If Head can lean on Heart and Gut to know that it is necessary to embrace change, then Head can flex its ideation muscle and help pave the way for solution-based thinking.

Heart is dreaming of more flexibility and time away from screens. Heart is the dreamer that is telling you that *life is out there waiting to be lived*, but Heart has to collaborate with Head and Gut to balance the needs and demands of our current realities. Heart sends your body messages when you have surpassed your screen time limit and need to recharge. Heart reminds you that too much of a good thing invokes the law of diminishing returns.

Gut hangs in the balance, enjoying the stability of something that it knows you are good at while also feeling absolutely sick when you have passed your computer limit. Gut grumbles about our adult responsibilities when Heart is asking us to go outside and play. Gut seeks a shift in the daily balance of analysis, computer time, self-care, and play.

EXISTENTIAL

What brings you joy, Maggie? The existentialists believe we are here to assign things meaning and to integrate that meaning into our lives. Lean into *fun* and *joy* to connect to your own sense of meaning and purpose in this life. If you are good at analysis and enjoy it, create a manifesto for that part of your life. Then honor the part of you (the very human part) that doesn't want to sit in front of a computer all day every day and write a manifesto for that, too. I believe that every struggle in our lives comes with a purpose, but we need to define that purpose for ourselves.

PROFESSIONAL

Since analysis is in your skill set, use it to your advantage when solving too much screen time. If you have a penchant for details, then flex that muscle to gather as much data as you can. Here is what I suggest:

- First, gather data on the situation (detailed below).
- Second, tease out what you have control over, where you have wiggle room, and what is completely out of your control.
- Third, start implementing experiments with the things you can control. Choose your top 5 ideas to influence your day. Start with just one small idea and then build from there.
- Reflect and repeat!

Consider this as a way of gaining detailed intel on your day:

- Keep a diary handy and record your mood and energy levels hourly.
- Maintain your research for at least 14 days.
- Do at minimum a weekly reflection on what you are learning, a daily one if you can:
  - At what point in your day do your eyes glaze over?
  - Do you experience any flow states? When and where do those occur?
  - When do you take breaks? What feels the most restorative?
  - How much do you engage with screens after work?
  - What changes do you have control over?

Keep a running list of what you have control over in your work and regarding screen time. Have at least three columns:

In my control, out of my control, and not sure or in the middle. For the things that are truly out of your control, do your best to let them go. Completely. Consider this a permission letter to totally ignore those annoying aspects of life that you can't do anything about. Let's focus on the other two areas: in your control and somewhere in the middle.

Brainstorming & Implementation

- Create a 100 ideas list (find it in your workbook): set a five-minute timer and write as many ideas as you can regarding spending less time on the computer, the ways that you recharge, and how you can implement more flexibility into your day.

- Choose your top 5 ideas from your 100 ideas list to try out a new approach.

- Use word association as another fun brainstorming tool. Start with one main concept in the center of your paper. For example, *Recharge from Screen Time* or *Recharge*. Then create a web of words around your bubble with associated ideas. Create three to four layers of associations, radiating out from the center. This practice usually results in all kinds of unexpected ideas.

Once you have plenty of ideas available to you and you have chosen your top 5, you can start designing some experiments to try out. Use the WOOP Worksheet in the downloadable workbook to help you design a foolproof plan. There is also a commitment contract available to you to put your commitment down in writing. This helps us psychologically commit more. I encourage you to try out one idea that you think will be the most fun to get you started. It's important that we celebrate all the small wins along the way to keep up the motivation.

An additional resource that can support your research and experimentation is taking the Sparketype Assessment. As a Certified Sparketype Adviser, I also recommend hiring a knowledgeable coach to help you work through all the steps. Knowing and understanding who you are, what motivates you, and what depletes you can support you in making some simple changes.

Don't give up Maggie! This is a real issue that so many of us grapple with these days. We must prioritize our health and well-being!

Avoid square eyes,

LARA

P.S. If you haven't read *The Boy with Square Eyes* by Juliet Snape, you might enjoy it! Also, check out *Rest as Resistance* at TheNapMinistry.com

ICE CREAM

What's the best flavor of ice cream?

Dear Best Flavor,

Haha, a challenge! I accept. I, too, struggle with these kinds of choices.

HEAD HEART GUT

Head says, *Let's make a list!* Chocolate, vanilla, cookie dough, duh.
    Heart votes for chocolate.
    Gut loves the rainbow.
    I'm getting a Head Heart Gut download, loud and clear: *How dare you! How could we ever choose just one?*

EXISTENTIAL

Best Flavor, you must explore and define the flavors of ice cream for yourself. Does there have to be just one? How might the answer to this question change your life?

PROFESSIONAL

I googly googled it, and I found the answer(s). They are ridiculously obvious, and it feels silly to write them here, but here we go:

Number one is vanilla ice cream. (BORING).

Second place is chocolate. (YUM).

What is your takeaway here?

Variety is spicey,

Lara

CREATIVE PASSIONS

Dear Lara,

How do I nurture my creative passions and pursue professional excellence while not sacrificing family time or growing resentful of missed opportunities? Your Best Brother-in-Law, Nick

Dear Nick,

Oh, sweet cheeks, you can't. One of life's greatest sorrows is not being able to live all the lives we envision for ourselves. With one choice, you pick a priority and discard another. That is the opportunity cost of all things. As a new-ish mom, I grieve the lives I have left behind. I grieve the lives I have discarded in favor of having children.

Resentment is part of life. Missed opportunities, too. Know that they are coming.

How can you prepare for their inevitable arrival? Perhaps knowing that obstacles are ever present can help you mitigate resentment by building a stronger inner compass. As they say in one of my favorite movies, *I Heart Huckabee's,* we are all drawn to "the inevitability of human drama."

What do you value most in life? And not just with your words, but with your *time*.

How do you take care of you when resentment comes banging heavy handed at the door? You nurture your creative passions through work and through family. You find little cracks in the scaffolding of daily life and squeeze creative passion out of or into them.

My heart hurts for you in this question. It's one of those harsh realities that you simply can't fit everything into every moment. There will be so many, countless really, missed opportunities.

You need to choose your priorities and choose them wisely.

HEAD HEART GUT

Head says, *Yes! We must figure this out!* And because you have an engineering mind, Head says, *Math and design will help us figure this out!*

Heart chuckles because the question is naively optimistic and while Heart wants a real answer, it already knows the truth. Then it feels the sting of oncoming tears. Heart knows the pain, the resentment, and the heartbreak of having to let go of one opportunity in favor of another.

Gut grumbles. Gut makes for an excellent guiding compass. Head will thwart Gut. Head will put Heart aside. Gut tumbles and turns to make itself heard. Gut likes the word *nurture* and gets excited about creative passions. Gut wants to be proud and strive for professional excellence. Gut grows warm around family. It's all an intricate puzzle that is built in real time. Heart and Gut want you to know that work is not everything, far from it actually. Science backs them up on this one.

EXISTENTIALISM

Regret research says that working too much is one of the top five regrets of the dying. Not being true to yourself and not nurturing relationships also made the list.

To re-write the capitalist script around work is a lifetime of work. Knowing this does not mean we turn around and suddenly work less. You are programmed to work as much as possible. Your self-worth depends on it. If you aren't actively re-writing the capitalist societal script that tells you you are worth what you produce, worth your productivity, your job, your salary, then it is taking you downstream with it. Even global culture says that you are worth what you get paid.

We measure our value as humans based on our performance and our likes and our reviews. Social media is the perfect example of this, illustrating our pleasure-seeking tendencies and our desire for approval. However, we've all experienced a time when we didn't get the response we wanted: a poor grade, a putdown by a peer, not receiving a raise or getting an unfavorable review at work. These soul crushing moments make us question our worth. It can be comical how quickly we get caught up in arbitrary measures of success. It's also totally normal.

But your paycheck and your work title are not your worth and do not help you determine a meaningful balance, Nick. How might you consider the regret of working too much alongside our social programming to seek status to create more balance in your own life?

A new script decoupling yourself from your work might include a list of personal experiences that you are most proud of and why. Consider what your greatest strengths are in your friendships and within your family. Who are you and what do you stand for without your material possessions? How do you live out your values through your experiences? A new script may be a reminder that you are not your work. For example, *I am not what I produce. I can control my actions, but not my outcomes. I am a loving partner and family member. I have a creative mind that I use to dream and build beautiful things. I appreciate the great outdoors, value the natural world, and seek to protect its resources.* Connecting to your own value as a human being can help build the compass to finding the balance you seek while also being the foundation of a rewarding life.

The urgency in life comes from the fact that you are going to die someday. Your creative passions pull at you; they play at your heartstrings. Your family, your community - those bring you happiness and meaning. Science shows us that our level of connection to our kin determines our level of happiness. Perhaps your happiness is not the defining factor of your life - it isn't for everyone. In that case, you have to decide - do you want to maximize your happiness? Your productivity? The work of a particular company? Further a particular cause? Do you want to center your life around family?

Nick, I'd like to encourage you to write a death letter to yourself. Allow me to explain. Write yourself a letter from the other side's perspective. You have died. What would your 20/20 hindsight be? What do you think that you truly want? What scares you about not being accomplished professionally?

Listen, you've got to dig deep. You've got to be honest with yourself. The problem with most people is that we aren't honest with ourselves. Humans haven't fully figured out why this is the case yet, but from what I have gathered, we are fearful, which ends up in poor decision-making, and ultimately, lack of awareness in how to develop personal honesty. For further research and insight into these phenomena, take a listen to the "You Can't Always Want What You Like" episode on *The Happiness Lab* podcast.

We probably aren't honest with ourselves because it can be painful and difficult, which are feelings we would rather avoid. Plus, since no one seems to teach emotional literacy past kindergarten, we may not even have the vocabulary and understanding to decipher our true emotions. This means that we must learn what we think and feel and be honest with ourselves.

For deepening your emotional and honesty journey, I highly recommend anything and everything by Brene Brown. Outside of reading all of Brene Brown's books and expanding your emotional repertoire, personal honesty comes with time and space reflecting on your thoughts, feelings, and experiences. Writing and talking things out can also be helpful. I suppose this is another reason people have a hard time being honest with themselves - the lack of any or all the aforementioned resources, including guidance, time, and information. Some people are born with a clearer or deeper understanding of themselves, but this is always a skill that can be cultivated and honed.

Can you imagine life without regrets? Well, that's a fantasy, not reality. Regrets are where we can do our deepest learning. It carves out an opportunity to make a significant change moving forward. If you find yourself missing family dinners, never being home for bedtime, and a resulting sense of loss, that's your internal values pointing the way to prioritize family time.

When you are feeling empty and restless, wishing you had more time to tinker around on creative projects, that's regret whispering *don't lose yourself*. Learn from that place. Live and breathe from that place. It's all that matters in the end.

PROFESSIONAL

Your professional excellence will serve you. You will be grateful for your professional development over time, as it will allow you greater freedom and flexibility throughout your life. Also, it will allow you to support the growth of whatever family you choose to have. However, careers and professional growth will gladly eat you whole. Careers are kind of like babies because they both want as much time and energy as you are willing to give them. But keep in mind that your intimate relationships are very different from those of an employer. Simone Stolzoff lays this out in his book *Good Enough Job*, showing us how modern societies overlap of home, work, and family can be incredibly fraught and downright destructive, especially to employees. My takeaway from Stolzoff's book is that boundaries matter, personal and professional. Figure out yours and make sure to implement them.

We still have so much to learn, we humans. We know already that working fewer hours and doing focused, energized activities leads to greater productivity. We have the power to create change. Great things are possible in shorter periods of time if we are present and focused on the task at hand.

You do not need to work a million hours to create good work and to grow professionally. Americans are *obsessed* with work, and we continue to elevate the workaholic more and more. Simone Stolzoff reviews this at length in his book, sharing statistics that illustrate how, despite America's growing wealth, we still work long hours with limited benefits and time off compared to other developed countries who have prioritized social support systems and more time off. Plus, there is solid evidence that working more hours does not make you a better or more productive worker. Stolzoff illustrates our skewed and confused values when he writes, "We shouldn't work less just because it allows us to be better workers. We should work less because it allows us to be better humans." America tends to frame everything within the context of work, but there is so much more to life than our professional development. Being a better human extends to every value that we hold, every relationship we engage in, and ultimately helps us build a better life, work included.

Additionally, as Oliver Burkeman points out in *4,000 Weeks: Time Management for Mortals*, work tends to lead to *more* work. Once you have cleared the decks, you have simply made space for the next long list of tasks that need to be completed. There is always more work to do.

Work is there, waiting.

Work is ready to go.

Whenever you want it, work is there.

There are always more opportunities than we can pursue.

When you feel resentment building, when you know you have missed an opportunity that you wanted - what questions can you ask to learn from the situation? What did you gain through your decision?

I also want you to know, Nick: you have got this. You are a hard worker. You're ambitious. Most importantly, *you care*. Caring is far more powerful than the ambition of professional success. As far as professional development and caring are concerned, it would be a beautiful thing if professionals integrated their *cares* about the world more into their work.

Do not worry so much about professional development. You may never be satisfied. Make sure you do not lay on your deathbed regretting that you worked so hard, missed time with your family, and allowed your creative hobbies to fall by the wayside. This is an extremely common regret, and it sneaks up on us! Since you are asking this question, you know already that our adult lives are a difficult balancing act. Here are my most practical tips for making space for creative passions, family, and work:

- Time chunk: schedule time for your hobbies and family, then respect your calendar! Plan the camping trip, share dinners at home with your family, do your best during the workday when you can.

- Do a quarterly review of your priorities, how you spent your time and how it felt. There are cycles when we need to work particularly hard, seasons we want to increase our time with loved ones, and times when we're bitten by the creative bug. Consider how much flexibility and control you have over your current schedule and try to make space for your current desires. Tip for planner lovers: the *Passion Planner* provides a monthly review with space for this specific activity!

- Do a little every day. The idea here is that giving even tiny amounts of time to something, say reading or connecting with your partner, adds up to a lot more than doing big bursts that feel overwhelming. So even if you only have half an hour to connect deeply with your child before bedtime or twenty minutes to give to a creative project, respecting that something is better than nothing. It will go a long way.

Embrace any missteps on your journey to answer this question. They are simply messages paving the way to greater clarity and balance.

Healing & resentful,

Lara

MAINTAIN

How do I maintain (or regain) my current high level of decisiveness, motivation, productivity, and energy?

Sincerely, Adam

Dear Adam,

If and when you find a thorough and effective answer to this question, you could make a lot of money on it as an online course! I say this both in jest and in complete seriousness. When we possess qualities like high levels of energy and motivation, others want to know how we got it and how to get it themselves. In the meantime, we can explore maintenance and energy generating activities that might help along the way.

HEAD HEART GUT

Head says, *YES! Great idea. We need to stay here and be productive, motivated, and decisive.*

Heart can be on board with this state, excited even. Heart knows that there are seasons of life and is equally interested in rest, rejuvenation, quiet, and contemplation.

Gut finds high energy levels very exciting. If Gut is aligned with Head and Heart, it can decipher if this high energy is useful, wise, good, just, and powerful. However, if Gut is not aligned, then it gets easily confused. Is Gut feeling good because it's checking boxes? Productivity for productivity's sake is not what humans are here for. We are not do-ings, we are be-ings. Gut can get caught up in all the decisiveness, thinking that it is doing worthwhile work from a productivity standpoint. Gut may need to recalibrate and remind Head about meaningful action from a values perspective.

EXISTENTIAL

I believe it to be completely natural that we want to maintain high levels of energy. Our current culture celebrates decisiveness, motivation, productivity, and energy. We praise people for these traits all the time. Capitalism teaches us that these traits are very important, essential even. And let's be honest, these states feel good for a reason! But not forever and not always. Our bodies tell us the true story. Our hearts and our souls know that these are not the whole picture. They do not define our existence.

I ask you, Adam, to write yourself a letter. If you could no longer share your amazing high energy with the world for a long time or even for the rest of your life, then what would your life be about? What do you share with those close to you? How else does your energy present itself?

There is something about the phrasing of your question that makes me want to remind you (and all readers) that you are not your productivity. It is such a difficult message to absorb that I believe it begs repeating.

PROFESSIONAL

The answer to your question varies depending on if you are maintaining or regaining. If you need to regain a high level of energy, I suggest you take thorough stock of where you are right now. Once you have an honest understanding of your current situation (which a coach can help you uncover if you're struggling!), then you can use various techniques to figure out which direction to go.

If you reflect on your life right now and find yourself burned out, I do not recommend taking further ambitious action. I recommend resting. Getting energy back usually means that you need rest. When we rest and do nothing, eventually, we are spurred to activity again.

It is core to my belief system that humans are not inherently lazy, but deeply creative, inspired beings. We *love* to do stuff! We love to make things. Humans have a deep need to create. However, many modern systems deplete us for a wide range of reasons.

If you are ready to proceed with regaining energy, here are a few exercises you can use to learn about how you personally recharge:

- Write about times you have felt depleted, followed by how you replenished your energy, or felt ready to be decisive and productive again.

- Reflect and define what you mean when you use words like "decisive" and "productive" (download the free Workbook for the Define My Terms Worksheet).

- Sign up for Oliver Burkeman's newsletter: The Imperfectionist.

- Do an energy audit to better understand your personal energy ebbs and flows (use the *Designing Your Life* Good Time Journal as one resource).

- Watch an inspirational video, like Mel Robbins's five-second-rule video.

- Dance it out.

- Research a coach who can help you go through these exercises and uncover what works best for you.

Don't worry, Adam! The sun will rise again. The seasons will turn. Your energy will rise. Respecting your own cycles will allow them to flow with the least amount of resistance. Learn from these things and share your wonderful gifts with the world.

In rest & regeneration,

LARA

HOLD TIGHT

How do I hold tight to what I learned throughout the pandemic, especially regarding the value of slowing way down, as the world returns to its overwhelming, demanding, and frenetic pace?

Dear Hold Tight,

I loved Julio Gambuto's article on the ultimate gaslighting post covid. Because it clearly lays out how we all want to feel good and normal in our daily lives again and that all the powers that be are going to capitalize on that desire. We don't want to be worrying about global tragedy and the complete failure of the systems we rely on. It's painful to live with the truth of Covid, all the grief and turmoil that it rained on our personal lives, on the economy, and the world at large. Gambuto lays out the good with the bad and how the return to normalcy will be an encouraged erasure of what happened during lockdown.

I really sense the desire and the underlying fear of this question. The desire to hold on, to not forget, to ingrain, integrate, and grow from your pandemic experience. This is so important. You have already done part of the work, which is recognizing that you have learned important lessons during the covid years, lessons worth holding on to. You are not alone, and the work you must do is a mission bigger than you and me. It is important to figure out how to integrate these lessons into your life, so you don't forget. We will explore how you can begin to continuously remind yourself.

HEAD HEART GUT

Head is scared. Head sees how the world is speeding back up and spinning ever faster. It's like the institutions that be want to move quicker now, as though there is something to catch up to. But there isn't. Head knows so many truths about the reality of the situation. Head knows that we have just experienced a major historical event. Head is confused because it struggles conceptualizing time. On top of all that, how did we really do lockdown?

Heart is scared. Heart experienced every up, every down, every complicated emotion. It experienced the ultimate roller coaster of Covid that somehow spanned years. Heart felt the greatest grief. Heart grieved the death of loved ones, the loss of freedom, the intense pain of many collective communities, and the failure of so many systems. It also felt the quiet, the slowdown, the rest. Heart closed down and Heart opened up. Heart says, *Remember these wonderful nuggets of wisdom.*

Heart wants you to remember that traffic stopped, and the air cleared, revealing scenic horizons that have been smog covered for decades. Heart wants you to remember how remote work, for better or worse, had a long-standing debut across industries and all kinds of jobs, formerly resisted and squashed by employers. Heart wants you to remember the community that was built between neighbors, the rekindled connections when you checked in on long-lost friends on zoom, or the new friends found on online dance parties and internet meetups. There is wisdom in all that happened and all that you experienced, Hold Tight. There is wisdom in the quiet, the clean air, the slowing down, and all that Covid revealed to us.

Gut is relaying Heart's roller coaster to Head. Gut senses the fear and is clutching on to that sense of slowing way down. Gut probably lives with a new level of anxiety that you have never experienced before. Gut is digesting the unprecedented, wild, seemingly impossible historical event that has unfolded for *years* now, killing approximately seven million people worldwide (with numbers continuously rising). It is more than any one body can take or fully understand. Take the time to slow down and boil a nice ginger tea for Gut. When you start to feel queasy, unstable, and anxious, that is Gut saying, *Can we take a minute to relax? How can we slow down?* Respect those messages by finding ways to embody slow practices, like having a cup of tea, journaling, or sitting quietly to admire a house plant.

EXISTENTIAL

The world, especially America, wants us to believe that something like a global lockdown is impossible. Something like COVID couldn't touch us. Until it did. The evidence is out there, but if you haven't seen, heard, or read it - or even if you have but willfully ignored it (like me), it's because that's what our dominant culture prefers. Humans still have a lot to learn about disaster and emergency preparedness, let alone prevention. National Geographic did a great job highlighting this topic as well as scientific publications like *Nature*, and popular books like *The Hot Zone* by Richard Preston. There is a wealth of knowledge and predictions of global pandemics strikingly similar to COVID-19 that are largely ignored by mainstream media.

The lock down years really showed us all that life is not as it seems. Anything is possible. Things can change for better and for worse. We operate so much on traditional principles. But it doesn't have to be that way. We can find new ways of being and living.

Existentialism is the philosophy that life is meaningless until we give it meaning. That means that we get to decide. We get to assign meaning to all the things that happen in our life. You are not alone, Hold Tight. Many of us have discovered that a slower pace of life is actually quite lovely. We learned that working from home could be brilliant or it could be a disaster. We saw that most things are indeed negotiable, but that we must stand firm with conviction. Consider the following questions:

- What does slowing way down look like for you?
- How can you mitigate the frenetic pace of life?
- What demands in your life are important?
- In what ways could they be altered to support your new-found wisdom?

Do not let the institutions at large gaslight you: you are not crazy, the pandemic lockdown did happen, there was good alongside the bad, and there are pieces of our transformation that are worth hanging on to. Yes, we want to return to a normal life, but we also want meaningful growth, for ourselves and our communities. I believe you learned many powerful things, and I hope that this response helps you fully integrate this wisdom.

PROFESSIONAL

In my experience, life gets increasingly complicated and fast-paced as we get older. At least as long as you let it. Based on the paths we have been put on and the ones we have chosen or crafted, we still have to deliberately pause to check that we're headed in a direction we actually want to go. For example, the school path for young adults in the western world is straightforward through grade school, on to college, maybe a master's degree and then employment.

To this day, one of my biggest regrets is not taking a gap year between high school and college. I had no idea what I wanted out of my college experience, and I think some time and space away from the normal path of my peers would have given me some room to figure out what suited me better. I was so dissatisfied with my college experience and so confused that I transferred three times, taking breaks in between semesters. It was an expensive disaster on all accounts.

I often think of salmon. Yes, the fish. You have to be a salmon in life. Salmon are a great illustration of the hero's journey in literature. Salmon are spawned upstream in freshwater, after which they head to the ocean for the majority of their lives. Then, when it is time for the salmon to mate and lay their eggs, the salmon return home to spawn and die.

Similarly, in a hero's journey, the main character is called to a transformational quest, often requiring them to leave home and go on an epic journey. They face many obstacles and are required to do many hard things to become a better version of themselves. After the hero has completed their quest, they return home to close the cycle.

Swimming upstream is a metaphor for going against the grain, the dominant culture. That is what is required of you, Hold Tight, if you wish to incorporate intentional slowness into your life. The dominant stream of the world currently is to go ever faster and to be expanding always. It's quite exhausting. As a salmon pursuing slowness, you'll have to use bursts of energy and strength to incorporate self-care and intentionality into your life. Use your inner compass to recognize safe havens and navigate a modern world ready to sweep you up in its fast current.

So much of culture, politics, and institutions are life pillars that have existed long before we had anything to say about it. Justice, living a good life, changing things for the better - all require us to be salmon. If we do not actively work for positive change and pay attention to how we want to live our lives, someone else will ultimately superimpose their ideas upon us.

If you have learned that slowing down is important to you, then embody the salmon. Here's my suggested approach to finding your inner salmon to integrate this learning:

- Write as much as you can about what you learned during the lockdown and our ongoing pandemic years.

- Paint, draw, make music, dance it out: use different forms to express your learning if you feel called to do so.

- As you find clarity in the lessons you learned and what exactly it is that you want to hang on to, condense the learning into one sentence. For example: slow way down or when I sit down to meditate every day, I feel like I can slow way down.

- Create rituals that embody these lessons and trigger those feelings in your body.

- Schedule time to remind yourself of what you learned, how to practice it, and to reflect on it to see if it is working.

Note here that slowing down is exactly what you need to do to integrate your learning. Slowing down to do each of these steps. Humans need to repeat things many times to learn thoroughly. We also need to contextualize things, build stories around them, and integrate them into our bodies.

Don't give up, Hold Tight.

Love, strength, & vigor,

Lara♥

Lara ♥

SUMMARY

While answering these Unanswersable Questions, a few important lessons stood out to me. They are a guide to living an authentic life.

PERSPECTIVE IS EVERYTHING

As I reflect on the questions we've traversed, I am reminded that this is not merely a book; it is a conversation, an exploration into what it means to be human. The interplay of mindfulness, relationships, career, and the mysteries of life and death forms a tapestry that captures the essence of our collective journey—a journey of self-discovery, connection, and the relentless pursuit of an authentic, meaningful life.

As rabble rousers participating in the quiet revolution of daily life, perspective is everything. The lens through which we view the world defines our reality. Intertwined with this understanding is the recognition that powerful reframes have the potential to reshape our entire existence. By altering our perspective, we wield the ability to change our reality. It's a profound realization that empowers us to navigate life's twists and turns with resilience and creativity.

At our core, we are seekers and creators. I believe that all humans generate their essence from that shared foundation. We are built to learn, grow, and create. We are fueled by an insatiable curiosity that modern life has a way of squashing. It is only through taking ownership of our perspectives that we can change our own realities.

LANGUAGE MATTERS

Language, the tool through which we articulate our thoughts and desires, assumes a pivotal role. Your language matters. The words you choose and how you use them are important. They shape your reality. Working with an effective coach can help us wield language more powerfully.

Our choice of words is important. Many of us use the same words but with a completely different meaning. For example: success, impactful, and enough. Getting really clear on what you want in life helps you understand yourself, measure progress, and know when you have accomplished something. This linguistic precision serves as a compass, guiding us toward a clearer understanding of our desires. By unraveling the intricacies of our language, we gain the ability to articulate our intentions with exactitude, aligning our thoughts with our actions.

MINDSET SHIFTS

Guided reflection helps us learn faster. Whether it is through journaling, meditation, or working with a coach, take the time to reflect on your life and ask big questions to help you grow. It shows the world that you care about being intentional and expanding your awareness. Mindset shifts, transformative as they are, rarely happen overnight. Instead, they require patience, persistence, and a conscious effort to cultivate new ways of thinking. Change is challenging. Yes, it's true that it is constant, but humans need the comfort of routine and structure, too. Change takes time and practice. That's why it is so important to cultivate patience and be kind to yourself. Regardless of the time it takes to build a new mindset, it is possible. Hold on and believe in the promise of change with practice.

Know that you are not alone. Give yourself permission to feel your feelings. Remember that your feelings do not define who you are. Share your authentic self with the world and build community to battle the ups and downs that are inevitable.

This book is a rallying cry for the rabble rousers, the dreamers, and the adventurers. Be creative, be bold.

May this not mark the end but the beginning of a new chapter in your own journey—one filled with purpose, connection, and the unwavering belief in the magic that resides within you. Celebrate yourself, heal yourself, invest in yourself, and, above all, take action. The world awaits your unique contribution to the symphony of life.

with love, strength, & vigor,

Lara Buelow

@LARABUELOW | APRIL 2022 | OPPORTUNITY KNOCKS

"Do not judge me by my success, judge me by how many times I fell down and got back up again." Nelson Mandela

BOOK CLUB QUESTIONS

- Which essay stands out to you the most? Why? What message or exercise are you taking away?

- Which essay is the most challenging for you and why? What parts do you struggle with the most? What feelings come up?

- Which section of the book feels most relevant to you?

- Which exercises feel the most impactful?

- Did reading the book impact your mood? If yes, describe how so?

- What aspects of the author's story could you most relate to and why? How did that make you feel?

- What new things did you learn about the way you use words/language?

- Which mindset shifts feel most relevant to your life?

- Describe three significant ah-ha's you had after reading this book.

- Describe three places where you got triggered.

- What was your biggest takeaway from the book?

THE POSTCARDS

To view the original postcards, click on this QR Code or visit Larabuelow.com/book/postcards

MUQPostcards

RESOURCES LIST

BOOKS

Atomic Habits by James Clear

Becoming by Michele Obama

The Body Keeps the Score by Besser Van Der Kolk

Books by Brene Brown

The Boy with Square Eyes by Juliet Snape

Calling in the One by Katherine Woodward Thomas

Chatter by Ethan Kross

The Complete Idiot's Guide to Awakening Your Spirituality by Jonathan Robinson

The Decision Book: 50 Models for Strategic Thinking by Mikael Krogerus and Roman Tschäppeler

Designing Your Life by Dave Evans & Bill Burnette

The Desire Map by Danielle LaPorte

Four Thousand Weeks: Time Management for Mortals by Oliver Burkeman

The Good Enough Job by Simone Stolzoff

The Life Changing Magic of Tidying Up by Marie Kondo

Never Split the Difference by Chris Voss

Peak Mind by Amishi Jha

Positive Intelligence by Shirzad Chamine

The Power of Regret by Daniel Pink

Rest is Resistance: A Manifesto by Tricia Hersey

The Second Brain by Micheal D. Gershon

Selfish, Shallow, and Self-absorbed: Sixteen Writers on the Decision to Not Have Kids, by Meghan Daum

Soul Pancake by Rainn Wilson

Sparked by Jonathan Fields

Tiny Beautiful Things by Cheryl Strayed

The Tools by Barry Michaels and Phil Stutz

The Top Five Regrets of the Dying by Bronnie Ware

The Wim Hof Method by Wim Hof

The Work by Bryon Katie

MEDIA

ARTICLES

The Big Quit https://www.nytimes.com/2021/11/05/opinion/great-resignation-quit-job.html

How to Feel Happier at Work When You Have the Urge to Quit by Christina Caron https://www.nytimes.com/2023/07/30/well/mind/work-stress-quitting.html

Male Friendships & Loneliness article https://www.nytimes.com/2022/11/28/well/family/male-friendship-loneliness.html?auth=login-googleitap&login=googleitap

Mauerpark Cafe San Francisco Closure https://hoodline.com/2020/08/mauerpark-the-castro-s-german-cafe-announces-permanent-closure/

Nature Communications article on decision-making: https://www.nature.com/articles/s41467-021-24907-x

The Harvard Study of Adult Development, Director Dr. Robert Waldinger, https://www.adultdevelopmentstudy.org/

How to Feel Happier at Work When You Have the Urge to Quit by Christina Caron https://www.nytimes.com/2023/07/30/well/mind/work-stress-quitting.html

What is the likelihood that you exist? https://www.sciencealert.com/what-is-the-likelihood-that-you-exist

Why is it so hard for me to make close friends? By Catherine Pearson https://www.nytimes.com/2022/11/28/well/family/male-friendship-loneliness.html?auth=login-google1tap&login=google1tap)

TOOLS

80,000 Hours

The Alliance Center, Denver, CO

BearCoaches.com

Bento Box

FutureMe.org, emails sent into the future

Freely, an anti-capitalist guide to pricing your work by Bear Hebert, an online course

Headspace app

Glassdoor

Know, Like, Trust (KLT) https://www.linkedin.com/pulse/know-like-trust-klt-trevor-johnson/

LinkedIN

Notion App https://www.notion.so/

Passion Planner by Angelina Trinidad

Resource Generation https://resourcegeneration.org/

Solidaire https://solidairenetwork.org/

Sovereign Dating Dating Coach Alana Mackenzie Page https://www.sovereign-dating.com/

Sustainable Connections, Bellingham, WA

VIDEO

I Heart Huckabees film

Priorities video: https://www.youtube.com/watch?v=cPgMeKfQFq8

The Rehersal with Nathan Fielder on HBO

Struthless on YouTube

PODCASTS

The Friendship Files with Julie Beck https://www.npr.org/2022/06/19/1106125372/after-years-of-interviews-julie-beck-has-defined-the-6-forces-that-fuel-friendsh

Finding Your Path Through Burnout: Sparked Podcast https://podcast.sparketype.com/finding-your-path-through-burnout-rediscovering-your-vitality/

The Happiness Lab with Dr. Laurie Santos

What Now? With Trevor Noah Trevor Noah's podcast

WEBSITES

Art by Lara Buelow www.artbylarabuelow.com

Better Health https://www.betterhelp.com/get-started/

Chinook Fund https://chinookfund.org/

Keep Writing Project with Hope Amico

Ocean Vuong https://www.oceanvuong.com/

ABOUT THE AUTHOR

As a certified coach and professional life designer, Lara Buelow is a catalyst for transformation. She specializes in guiding professional women through powerful career transitions, empowering them to become their most effective, fulfilled selves. With a talent for helping clients get unstuck and reignite their passions, Lara infuses her coaching with a contagious zest for life. She firmly believes that joy and purpose should be integral to success, encouraging clients to have more fun, chase their dreams, and rediscover their sense of purpose.

Hailing from picturesque Germany and sunny California, Lara blends nature's inspiration with coastal vibrancy in her coaching. Leading creative programs remotely, her wisdom transcends boundaries.

Lara lives in Colorado with her husband, Adrian, and their two children. When she's not parenting or coaching, she gets lit up by reading, writing, exercising, and spending quality time outside with friends. She also loves to indulge in surfing ankle-biter waves, painting murals on whatever walls friends or family can offer, and dancing at concerts. Lara frequently spends time in California with her side of the family breathing in the coastal air.

Lara's clients uncover not just career clarity but also a renewed sense of self, equipped to navigate life's twists and turns. If you're ready to transform your career and embrace a purposeful, fun-filled life, Lara Buelow is the coach to light your path to success. Lara can be reached at larabuelow.com.

WORK WITH LARA

L ara offers *Designing Your Life* coaching to people all over the country. She also offers group programs and private coaching.

That Moxie Life is Lara's signature month-long challenge. It focuses on building your fun muscle and incorporating more adventure into your life. Sign up for Lara's newsletter to stay informed.

Lara is certified in the Sparketype content from Jonathan Fields *Good Life Project*. The Sparketype Assessment is a free personality strengths profile to highlight exactly what lights you up in life and work. Lara is certified to coach individuals and groups through the Sparketype content. For more information, visit www.sparketype.com or reach out to Lara@LaraBuelow.com

Lara's Art Website: http://www.artbylarabuelow.com/

For a complimentary clarity call, visit LaraBuelow.com

Printed in the USA
CPSIA information can be obtained
at www.ICGtesting.com
LVHW070527140824
787855LV00005B/7